WOMEN OF THE FRENCH REVOLUTION

'What struck me was the air of general benevolence. Selfishness seemed banished from every heart. There was no longer a distinction between classes. People jostled together talking to one another as though they were one family . . .'
> – Théroigne de Méricourt, speaking of Paris in the early days.

'Women awake! The tocsin of enlightenment and reason resounds through the universe; recognise your rights.'
> – Olympe de Gouges, 1791.

'A feeling of indescribable happiness came over me. Seated opposite my husband, whose life I was saving, with my two children on my knee, everything seemed possible. Poverty, work, misery, nothing was too difficult with him beside me.'
> – Madame de la Tour du Pin, escaping with her family to America, March 1794.

In this fascinating and moving account, Linda Kelly follows the fortunes of some of the leading women of the day to give a fresh slant to the dramatic, and later shattering, events of the French Revolution.

Linda Kelly's earlier books are *The Marvellous Boy*, a study of the poet Thomas Chatterton, *The Young Romantics*, and *The Kemble Era*. She has also co-edited two anthologies, *Feasts* and *Proposals*.

D0088428

HAMISH HAMILTON PAPERBACKS

*For a complete list of available
titles see the end of this book*

Women of the French Revolution

by

LINDA KELLY

A HAMISH HAMILTON PAPERBACK
London

HAMISH HAMILTON LTD

Published by the Penguin Group
27 Wrights Lane, London W8 5TZ, England
Viking Penguin Inc, 40 West 23rd Street, New York, New York 10010, U.S.A.
Penguin Books Australia Ltd, Ringwood, Victoria, Australia
Penguin Books Canada Ltd, 2801 John Street, Markham, Ontario,
Canada L3R 1B4
Penguin Books (N.Z.) Ltd, 182–190 Wairau Road, Auckland 10, New Zealand

Penguin Books Ltd, Registered Offices: Harmondsworth, Middlesex, England

First published in Great Britain 1987 by
Hamish Hamilton Ltd
First published in this edition 1989

Copyright © 1987 by Linda Kelly

3 5 7 9 10 8 6 4 2

The author would like to thank Felice Harcourt and the Harvill Press for
permission to quote from her translation of the Memoirs of Madame de la
Tour du Pin on pages 16, 26 and 77.

Except in the United States of America, this book is sold subject
to the condition that it shall not, by way of trade or otherwise, be lent
re-sold, hired out, or otherwise circulated, without the
publisher's prior consent, in any form of binding or cover other than
that in which it is published and without a similar condition
including this condition being imposed on the subsequent purchaser.

ISBN 0–241–12677–0

Typeset at The Spartan Press Ltd
Printed in Great Britain by
Cox and Wyman Ltd, Reading, Berks.

To Marie Noële Kelly

List of Illustrations

Madame de Staël, March of the Women on Versailles, Théroigne de Méricourt, by kind permission of the Bulloz Picture Agency, Paris.

Madame de la Tour du Pin, by kind permission of Count Christian de Liederkerke-Beaufort.

Olympe de Gouges, "Club patriotique des femmes", A Republican divorce, by kind permission of the Giraudon Picture Agency/Musée Carnavalet, Paris.

Madame Roland, Madame Tallien, Joséphine de Beauharnais, by kind permission of the BBC Hulton Picture Library, London.

"Woman has the right to mount the scaffold . . ." by kind permission of the British Library, London.

"Merveilleuses et Incroyable", Revolutionary fashion, by kind permission of the Mansell Picture Collection, London.

Preface

"O my poor sex," wrote the feminist playwright Olympe de Gouges, "O women who have gained nothing from the Revolution!" In 1789 the Declaration of the Rights of Man gave women for a fleeting moment the hope that its clauses might extend to them as well. (Olympe de Gouges' Declaration of the Rights of Woman was the expression of that hope.) In the same year, 1789, women marching on Versailles brought back the King and royal family to Paris. In the crowd scenes of the Revolution, where numbers were of prime importance, women, for a short time, had a powerful influence on events. Women's clubs and "fraternal" or mixed clubs, where women were admitted on equal terms with men, provided a forum for their views on politics and social questions. Women's education was considered on a national basis. The aim of education, wrote Condorcet in his report to the Convention on the subject, was to "offer to all the individuals of the human race the means to supply their needs, to ensure their well being, to know and exercise their rights and to understand and carry on their duties".

By the end of 1793 the bright hopes of the Revolution had been dimmed. Condorcet, the champion of women, not only in his views on education but in his call for women's suffrage, *Sur l'admission des femmes au droit de cité* was in hiding; the idea of equal opportunities in education for women had been dismissed as a chimera. Olympe de Gouges, having tempted fate in offering to appear at the trial of the King in his defence, had gone to the scaffold. Women's clubs had been suppressed and the right to assemble in the streets denied; the mob, so vital in the early stages of the Revolution, was a threat to the government it had helped to bring to power. From then on women might be goddesses of Reason; they could no longer interfere in public life.

The question of women's rights, briefly raised in the Revolution and forgotten for most of the century thereafter, was never an important issue for most women of the time. (It was not until 1946 that women in France obtained the vote.) Those like Madame de Staël and Madame Roland, with the authority and standing to influence ideas, held no brief for the other members of their sex. Passionately interested in power, they chose to exert it behind the scenes, disclaiming – not always convincingly – all political ambitions for themselves. Olympe de Gouges and others, debarred by their lack of education and their dubious social status, had never any real chance of being heard.

In 1854 Michelet published his *Femmes de la Révolution*, a gallery of portraits – "*quelques héroïnes, quelques femmes plus ou moins célèbres*" – collected and expanded from his history of the French Revolution. It was the first serious attempt to look at women's participation in the Revolution, though for Michelet it remained unthinkable that women should share political responsibility with men. "It is not our fault," he wrote, "if nature has made women, if not feeble at least infirm, subject to periodic illnesses, creatures of emotion, children of the sidereal world, hence unfitted by their uneven constitutions to undertake the functions of political societies."

Michelet's views reflected the prejudices of his time; they had not changed much from those of sixty years before. It was not until the end of the nineteenth century that Léopold Lacour, in his *Trois Femmes de la Révolution*, gave the first detailed and sympathetic account of the feminist movement as exemplified by Olympe de Gouges, Théroigne de Méricourt and Claire Lacombe, leader of the most influential woman's club of the Revolution, the Républic-aines Révolutionnaires. Since then, especially in recent years, there have been a number of important studies of the role of women in the Revolution, most notably Paule Marie Duhet's *Les Femmes et la Révolution*, and *Women in Revolutionary Paris*, a selection of documents, translated with notes and commentary by Darline Gay Levy and others. These are invaluable sources; the story of feminism in the Revolution, confused and ultimately unsuccessful, has been one of my subsidiary themes.

My chief concern, however, has been with individuals. Remarkable events throw up remarkable characters and, as Carlyle puts it, all men love to know their fellow men, or in this case women, in singular situations. At every stage of the Revolution women, to a greater or lesser extent, were associated with its main events. Their experiences, often tragic, sometimes heroic, illuminate the history of the period and incidentally throw a light on women's lot in general at the time.

The cast of characters in the French Revolution is enormous – "worse than a Russian novel," said Lord Clark. Even among women the choice is considerable. Taking the chronology of the Revolution as my central thread I have concentrated on those who, at least at the outset, were sympathetic to its aims. Thus the Queen, for the purposes of this study, appears only in relation to the other characters; the heroism of the Princesse de Lamballe, the martyrdom of the Carmelite nuns, have no place in this narrative. My sole exception is Madame de la Tour du Pin: an aristocrat without political pretensions, her memoirs give fascinating glimpses of some of the key moments of the Revolution and her deepening response to its dramas.

Other characters cover the revolutionary spectrum. Madame de Staël was allied with those liberal aristocrats, Narbonne and Talleyrand among them, who sought a constitutional monarchy for France. Madame Roland was the inspiration of the Girondins, a republican who found herself outstripped by the fanaticism of the left. Thérésia Cabarrus, associated with the Terror through her lover Tallien, was saved from the guillotine by his overthrow of Robespierre; she was greeted on her emergence from prison as Notre Dame de Thermidor. Théroigne de Méricourt was the legendary incarnation of the mob. Her figure, in its scarlet riding habit, flashes through the crowd scenes of the Revolution and is evoked by Baudelaire in a memorable quatrain:

Avez vous vu Théroigne, amante de carnage,
Excitant à l'assaut un peuple sans souliers,
La joue et l'oeil en feu, jouant son personnage,
Et montant, sabre au poing, les royaux escaliers. ★

Olympe de Gouges was the heroine of the cause of women's rights. Charlotte Corday, appearing briefly at the centre of the stage, won immortality and death by her assassination of Marat. Finally Joséphine de Beauharnais, no heroine but a survivor, came through the Terror and imprisonment to become a leader of the corrupt and pleasure loving society that grew up after Robespierre's fall. Her marriage to Bonaparte, on the eve of his departure for Italy, effectively closes the story of the Revolution and opens the way to the Napoleonic era.

★Have you seen Théroigne, lover of carnage,
Urging a crowd without shoes to the assault,
Her cheek and eye on fire, playing out her role,
And mounting, sabre in hand, the royal stairway.

Chapter 1

On May 4, 1789, the representatives of France's three estates, Clergy, Nobility and Third Estate, marched in procession through the streets of Versailles to a solemn mass in preparation for the opening of the States General the next day. Twelve hundred strong, they wore the dress of their respective orders, the plain black suits and *tricornes* of the Third Estate in sober contrast to the silks and plumes of the nobility, the violet vestments of the bishops, and the splendour of the royal cortege, King, Queen and Court, whose last great gala this would be.

Versailles was *en fête*, the balconies hung with tapestries, the broad streets filled to overflowing with the crowds who had flocked from Paris for the great procession. It was a momentous occasion. The States General had not met since 1614. Summoned in response to overwhelming economic pressures, they carried with them the hopes of the nation who saw in their foregathering not only the prospect of financial salvation but the opening of a new and golden age.

From a window along the crowded route the Swedish ambassadress, Madame de Staël, a plain young woman with brilliant dark eyes, stood watching with a group of friends. For her, above all, it was a thrilling moment. The States General were meeting under the aegis of her father, the Finance Minister, Jacques Necker, recalled to power just nine months earlier. So great had been her pleasure at his reinstatement, after eight years out of office, that in walking home through the Bois de Boulogne on the evening of his appointment she had been convinced she would be attacked by robbers. Such joy, she felt, must have its counterpart in some great misfortune.

She was not robbed, though destiny, she noted later, would amply justify her fears. Meanwhile, despite the country's desperate economic situation, exacerbated by bad harvests and an exceptionally hard winter that year, she shared the almost universal optimism and excitement that greeted the opening of the States General. Years later, in her last great book, *Considérations sur la Révolution française*, she recalled the opening procession. It was an imposing spectacle, decked out in all the pageantry of the *ancien régime*. But it was on the members of the Third Estate, in whose hands, it already seemed clear, lay the future of the coming assembly, that she focused her attention. Here for the first time were the elected representatives of the people, their powers as yet untried but already set out in the famous pamphlet of the Abbé Sieyès: "What is the Third Estate? Everything. What has it been in the political order hitherto? Nothing. What does it seek to become? Something." Few of the individual deputies, for the most part lawyers, businessmen and journalists, were yet known to the public. One figure stood out vividly among them, a nobleman who had thrown in his lot with the Third Estate, the Marquis de Mirabeau. Notoriously immoral, strikingly ugly, with a massive head and vast dishevelled mane of hair, his whole personality, wrote Madame de Staël, seemed stamped with the power of a tribune of the people.

"I was standing," she continued, "at the window next to the wife of the Foreign Minister, Madame de Montmorin, and I expressed, I must confess, the liveliest hopes at this first sight of the nation's representatives in France. Madame de Montmorin was by no means a clever woman but she said in a decided tone which nonetheless impressed me: 'You are quite wrong to rejoice. Great disasters for France and for ourselves will be the consequence of this.'" The unfortunate woman, as Madame de Staël recorded, spoke more truly than she knew. Together with all her family she would perish in the Revolution.

In May 1789 such tragedies seemed unthinkable. The century now approaching its last decade – the century of enlightenment and reason – seemed to be approaching its climax and fulfilment. In every branch of France's intellectual life new ideas had changed the expectations of the age, undermining its institutions without as yet destroying them. Still possessing the privileges of the past but filled with generous aspirations for the future, the liberal aristocracy stood poised between two eras. It was an enchanted if delusory lull. "If I by sacrificing the memory of that brief period of light and glory," wrote Talleyrand long after, "could add ten years to my life *now* I would not do it."

Thirty-five years old at the outset of the Revolution, Talleyrand was one of Madame de Staël's closest circle, indeed at one time one of her lovers. Madame de Staël's husband, the Baron de Staël Holstein, was already more or less discounted by his wife. In 1789, moreover, she was in the first flush of her love for Louis, Comte de Narbonne Lara, a well known breaker of hearts, given further glamour by his rumoured royal birth – he was commonly supposed to be the son of Louis XV. A boon companion of Talleyrand, his extravagance and dissipation had hitherto kept him from any serious post. Caught up in the wake of Madame de Staël, and fired with genuine idealism, he now sought a wider stage for his abilities.

Madame de Staël was never a beauty. Stocky, with heavy almost masculine features, her chief assets were her fine dark eyes and handsome arms and bosom, always lavishly displayed. But she made her looks forgotten and inspired an illustrious string of lovers by the fascination of her conversation. It was an art in which the salons of the eighteenth century excelled, and to which she brought an eloquence and emotional intensity that foreshadowed the romanticism of the nineteenth. "If I were Queen," said a contemporary, "I would command her to talk to me always." There were some who found her brilliance exhausting. "Her works are my delight," wrote Byron, who knew her in her later years, "and so is she – for half an hour."

In 1789 her career as a writer – the author of *Delphine, Corinne* and *De l'Allemagne* – still lay before her, though an essay on Rousseau published privately the previous year had won her a certain reputation in the world of letters. But she was already a figure at the centre of events. In her salon at the Swedish embassy all the energy of liberty, as she expressed it, was combined with all the graces of the *ancien régime*. Social barriers to a large extent were broken down, politicians, noblemen and men of letters mingled, though Madame de Staël, always conscious of her somewhat invidious position as the daughter of the Swiss banker Necker, had a special penchant for members of France's noblest and most ancient families, Narbonne and Talleyrand among them. With her father now the hero of the moment and Narbonne as her acknowledged lover, her social ambitions seemed at their zenith.

She listened with pride when her father at the opening of the States General the next day gave a three hour speech on the state of the nation's finances – his voice running out half way through, he was forced to have the rest of it read by a substitute. The fact that his speech was totally uninspiring and in no way corresponded to the wider aims of the assembly was something her memoirs pass over. For Madame de Staël her father, still more than any of her lovers, was the idol of her adoration.

★　★　★

For another member of the audience, Madame de Gouvernet – better known from her memoirs as Madame de la Tour du Pin* – Necker's speech, with its drone of figures and statistics, had been a long ordeal of boredom. A lady in waiting to the Queen, she had sat with the other ladies of the court in the front row of a tier of benches with nothing but the knees of those behind to support her. "To my nineteen year old ears," she wrote, "the speech seemed never ending. I don't think I've ever felt so weary in my life." But she observed the rest of the proceedings with a lively eye: the murmur of revulsion as Mirabeau took his place among the other deputies, the ceremonial entrance of the King. "This good prince," she noted, "was not dignified in his appearance. He stood badly

*Her husband, the Comte de Gouvernet, inherited the title of Comte de la Tour du Pin de Gouvernet on his father's death in 1794; he was created Marquis de la Tour du Pin in 1820.

and walked with a waddle; his movements were abrupt and lacking in grace; his sight was poor and since it was not customary to wear spectacles he screwed up his face." The Queen on the other hand was a figure full of grace and dignity, "but it was plain from the convulsive way she used her fan that she was very agitated. She often looked towards that part of the chamber where the Third Estate was sitting, and seemed to be trying to pick out a face in the ranks of that mass of men amongst whom she already had so many enemies."

In direct contrast to Madame de Staël, whom she nonetheless liked and admired, Madame de la Tour du Pin had no political or intellectual pretensions. Although not strictly beautiful, her pale blonde hair and dazzling complexion made her one of the most attractive ladies of the court. Devoted to her husband, whose father was shortly to become Minister of War, she took no part in the love affairs and intrigues that were so much a part of the aristocratic life of the time. "Madame de Gouvernet is impossible," said Talleyrand's brother, the Prince de Périgord, "she treats all young men as though they were her brothers."

This unfashionable fidelity never failed to astonish Madame de Staël. Her own husband had married her blatantly for money; she, as a Protestant, excluded from marriage into the Catholic aristocracy, had chosen him for the social base his embassy and title provided. Handsome, well spoken, he had "all the qualities needed in a man one cannot love"; she asked little more from the bargain. Already embarked on a life-long career of seeking love elsewhere, she was primly judged by Madame de la Tour du Pin. "Her great qualities," she wrote, "were no more than tarnished by those passions to which she abandoned herself the more easily because she felt a pleasant surprise whenever a man sought from her those pleasures from which her unfortunate looks seemed to have debarred her for ever. Indeed I have every reason to suppose that she surrendered herself without the slightest struggle to any man who showed himself more aware of her physical than her intellectual charms."

Through the months leading up to the opening of the States

General Madame de la Tour du Pin had done her best to avoid the political discussions which had become the main preoccupation of the day. Young and pretty, she was bent on enjoyment in a society eminently fitted to provide it. Almost the last event she records before the opening of the States General was a grand ball given by the Duke of Dorset at the British Embassy. Supper was served at little tables in a gallery whose walls were completely covered with foliage. The invitation cards had read: "Ladies will wear white". With Irish contrariness – her family, the Dillons, were "wild geese" from the reign of James II – she appeared in blue from top to toe, with blue flowers in her corsage, blue ribbons on her gloves, blue feathers in her powdered hair. "This small revolt," she wrote, "earned me a certain success in society, and people did not fail to quote the song 'Blue bird, blue skies'. Even the Duke of Dorset was amused and remarked that the Irish were always an unruly race."

In this light-hearted manner, "laughing and dancing our way to the precipice", Madame de la Tour du Pin approached the month of May. "Thinking people," she wrote, "talked only of abolishing abuses. France, they said, was about to be reborn. The word Revolution was never uttered. Had anyone used it they would have been thought mad."

* * *

With the opening of the States General Madame de Staël moved the centre of her social operations to Versailles. Here, in the sumptuous reception rooms of the Contrôle Général or Treasury, her parents' official residence, she flung herself into the task of furthering her father's interests by every means that intrigue, talk and force of personality could devise. Her mother, Madame Necker, increasingly troubled by nerves and ill health, was content to move into the background, leaving it to her daughter to welcome Necker's supporters, moderate liberals like himself, and those more extreme to the left or right who might be won round to his views. Distrusted at court, too cautious for the bolder elements of the Third Estate, Necker had taken on the role of Finance Minister with grave misgivings. "The daughter of a Minister," he told Madame de Staël, "has nothing but pleasure from the reflection of her father's power. But the power itself, especially in times like these, is a terrible responsibility."

Madame de Staël was more sanguine than her father. From the earliest age she had been brought up to believe in his genius as an article of faith. An only child, educationally force-fed by her mother, she had grown up amidst the intellectual élite of Paris, drawn to her parents' salon by the aura of power, financial and political, that surrounded her father. The gatherings would be orchestrated by Madame Necker round her husband, whose very silences would be treated as evidence of profundity. "See, he is thinking," she would murmur to her guests when Necker, ponderous and solemn, fell into an Olympian reverie. If there were some who secretly mocked the mutually admiring couple there were few who dared by-pass them at a time when economic problems had come to dominate French life, and when Necker, with his formidable knowledge of banking and the laws of credit, seemed to hold the key to their solution.

Now more than ever this opinion persisted. Throughout France Necker was regarded as a potential saviour, his likeness reproduced in countless prints and portrait busts, his popularity almost equal to the King's. Except in private he kept his doubts to himself. "His looks, his address etc., say *I* am the man," wrote an American visitor Gouverneur Morris, adding drily, "if he really is a great man I am deceived."

An experienced observer of foreign affairs, who had sat in the American Senate, Gouverneur Morris had arrived in Paris earlier that year as an agent for his family business. Fluent in French, and armed with letters from General Washington, he had quickly made his way into the leading salons of the day, Madame de Staël's and her mother's among them. "She is a woman of marvellous wit, and above all vulgar prejudices," he wrote to Washington. "Her salon is something like the temple of Apollo."

The chief model for Necker and his liberal supporters, as they

7

envisaged France's future, was a constitutional monarchy along English lines. It was an ideal his daughter wholeheartedly supported. Never a democrat, she advocated a two chamber system, with an upper chamber consisting of France's highest and most ancient nobility, heirs and trustees of the country's great traditions. Its leading members, it went without saying, were to be found among her friends.

It was a solution which on paper had almost everything to recommend it. Twenty-five years later, as she recorded in her *Considérations sur la Révolution française*, it was adopted more or less in its entirety by Louis XVIII. But neither the King, conditioned to a wholly different view of kingship, nor the Third Estate, now demanding that the States General should vote as a single assembly, were prepared to countenance such an arrangement. From the first the overwhelming issue confronting the States General had been the question of representation: with twice the members of the other two orders, the Third Estate could only dominate if the voting was by head, and not by separate estates. While Louis XVI dithered and Necker offered compromise solutions, the Third Estate took the law into their own hands. On June 17 they unilaterally declared themselves to be the nation's representatives, adopting the title of the National Assembly; they confirmed their determination three days later in the Tennis Court oath.* A trickle, then a flood from the other two orders joined them. On June 27, having lost all the credit he would have gained by accepting it freely, the King was forced to recognise a *fait accompli*.

Meanwhile the position of Necker, cast by the King's supporters as the architect of his defeat, was growing more and more untenable. He had tried to resign but had withdrawn his resignation at the royal request for fear of provoking popular disorder. But from day to day, he told his daughter, he expected to be arrested, and his worst fears seemed confirmed when the King, in

---

*Finding themselves locked out of the hall where they habitually met, the deputies had repaired to an indoor tennis court nearby where they swore not to separate until the Constitution had been established.

an attempt to reassert his authority, drew up troops round Paris and Versailles. On July 11, as Necker was sitting at dinner, he was handed a note from the King. He read it without a word; at the end of dinner, when his guests had left, he ordered his carriage and without even pausing to pack set out with his wife towards the frontier. The King had dismissed his Finance Minister, enjoining him to leave the country secretly in order to avoid a public outcry. Loyal to her father, and dragging her reluctant husband from his diplomatic duties, Madame de Staël joined her parents in Brussels two days later. From there they set out for Switzerland and it was on the road to Basel, five days after it had taken place, that they first heard the news of the fall of the Bastille.

Chapter 2

In the gardens and arcades of the Palais Royal, where a very different world from that of court or salons had its existence, the news of Necker's dismissal had been received with fury and consternation. The purlieus of the Duc d'Orléans, well known for his hostility to the King and his friendliness to new ideas, the Palais Royal had long been a hotbed of political discussion and dissent. It was an area of brothels, restaurants and gambling houses, where courtesans brushed skirts with fashionable ladies and where would-be politicians found a ready audience in the crowds that gathered there for pleasure and, increasingly, for the latest political news. In the months of mounting excitement and unrest leading up to the fall of the Bastille a stream of political tracts and newspapers poured out from the print shops almost unchecked, while in coffee houses and outdoor cafés impromptu orators leapt on chairs and tables to denounce the government and propound their views.

It was one such orator, Camille Desmoulins, an impecunious young lawyer with lank hair and an ugly clever face who, leaping up onto a chair and brandishing a pair of pistols gave the signal for the attack on the Bastille. Necker's dismissal, he announced, was the "tocsin for a new Saint Bartholomew", patriots were about to be massacred, it was time to sound the call to arms. Pinning a piece of green ribbon on his hat – "the colour of hope" and incidentally of Necker's livery – he called on the crowd to show their allegiance to the common cause by wearing a similar cockade. Within minutes the trees of the Palais Royal were stripped of their foliage as his enthusiastic listeners adorned their hats with branches, and re-peating his cry "to arms" surged from the Palais Royal into the streets, bearing the busts of Necker and the Duc d'Orléans, looted from a nearby waxworks, before them.

Such at least, unconfirmed by any other contemporary account, was Camille Desmoulins' description of his role in sparking off the mob activity which two days later would culminate in the storming of the Bastille, the massacre of the governor and most of the garrison, and the release of the seven prisoners who were all that were left in this fabled bastion of tyranny. In giving, as he called it, the "signal for the Revolution", he took his first step from obscurity into the limelight.

An event so vast in its symbolic significance as the fall of the Bastille created its own legends almost simultaneously. Camille Desmoulins, with the help of his persuasive pen, took his part in its mythology. So too did the woman who would come to personify the fury of the Revolution, a fury in action as he was in words, the *belle Liégoise*, Théroigne de Méricourt.

Born near Liège – she took her name from her native village of Marcourt – Théroigne de Méricourt had arrived in Paris the previous year under the protection of an elderly nobleman, the Marquis de Persan, and set up house near the Palais Royal. Attracted by the Revolution "as a moving object is sucked in by a whirlwind", she had passed the summer months in the thick of the political debates that made the Palais Royal a rival to the National Assembly. Though she denied having taken part in the storming of the Bastille she was cast in the eyes of her contemporaries, and of historians from Lamartine to Carlyle, as a symbol of the people's vengeance, a virago urging on the mob.

"From the first moment of the uprising," wrote Lamartine in his *Histoire des Girondins*, "she descended into the streets. Her beauty was like a banner to the multitude. Dressed in a blood red riding habit, her sabre by her side, two pistols at her waist, she flew to the forefront of the fray. She was in the van of those who forced the gates of the Tuileries and carried off the cannon, first too in the assault which scaled the towers of the Bastille. The victors awarded her a sword of honour in the breach."

Her real involvement with the Revolution was more gradual and less dramatic. Barely educated, she had trained as a singer in England and had made her way through a combination of beauty, wit and talent to that shadowy area between the arts and the demi-monde. She was now twenty-eight, small, dark-haired, with piquant, slightly battered features and "one of those *retroussé* noses that change the fate of empires". Despite an inevitably dubious past – and an income from the Marquis de Persan – she was in no way free and easy with her favours. Her passion would be politics, not love. In 1789, however, her political indoctrination had only just begun. Her first training would be in the Palais Royal and recalling it two years later, she speaks movingly of the atmosphere there during those early months when hope and idealism were as much in evidence as incipient violence.

"What struck me most was the air of general benevolence. Selfishness seemed banished from every heart. There was no longer a distinction between classes. People jostled together, talking to one another as though they were one family. The rich, at this moment of fermentation, mixed voluntarily with the poor and did not disdain to speak to them as equals. People's very expressions seemed changed."

And later, in attending the sessions of the National Assembly at Versailles, we see her democratic ardour growing.

"At first," she wrote, "I understood little of their deliberations but gradually I came to see the light and at last to realise that here were the People confronted face to face with Privilege. My sympathy for their cause increased as I grew better informed and transformed itself into ardent love as I became persuaded that right and justice were on the People's side."

Now in the wake of the fall of the Bastille, the news of which had made her weep for joy, she took part in the public celebrations which accompanied Louis XVI's ceremonial entry into Paris on July 17. "I was marching in the crowd before him," she wrote. Dressed in "a white riding habit, with a round hat", she joined in the shouts and plaudits of the spectators as, standing on the balcony of the Hôtel de Ville and wearing a tricolour cockade, the King gave his public (if privately reluctant) assent to the triumph of the Revolution.

* * *

On July 20, yielding to *force majeure*, the King recalled Necker to power. His return to Paris was triumphal. All along his route he was greeted as a hero; cheering citizens drew his carriage through the towns on their way, women working in the fields fell to their knees as he passed by. In Paris the popular enthusiasm reached its height.

"May I be permitted to linger yet once more on the memory of that day," wrote Madame de Staël, "the last of perfect happiness in my life. . . . The whole population of Paris was crowded in the streets; from windows and rooftops men and women were crying 'Long live Necker!' When he approached the Hôtel de Ville the acclamations redoubled; the whole great square was filled with a multitude all animated by a single sentiment, all pressing on the footsteps of one man – and that man was my father."

When Necker, appearing on the balcony of the Hôtel de Ville, addressed the crowd, enjoining peace and reconciliation amongst all parties, he was greeted with still further transports. "I knew no more," wrote Madame de Staël, "for at that moment I lost consciousness, overwhelmed by an excess of joy."

Necker had returned to Paris to face a situation of near anarchy. Law and order had broken down, violence was erupting all over France in what came to be known as the Great Fear. Meanwhile bankruptcy threatened the country, bread shortages were becoming acute, there were food riots in the streets of Paris. "I feel," he had written to his brother before accepting his recall, "as if I were approaching an abyss."

In fact he was to become increasingly irrelevant to the fast moving march of events in France. His appearance on the balcony had marked the climax of his popularity; from then on it would only decline. Power had moved into the hands of the National Assembly, more and more a law unto itself. The following month saw the heady night of August 4 when, in one unforgettable session the nobility renounced their ancient rights and privileges, dismantling the feudal system at one stroke. In a similar exalted spirit, while France's problems multiplied, the deputies addressed themselves to discussing and promulgating the Declaration of the Rights of Man. It was published later in the month but the King – still so central to the system that his assent, wrote Madame de Staël, would have been sought to the creation of a republic – at first refused to ratify it. He would do so finally on October 5. It was his last day but one in Versailles, the last day but one of the French monarchy's life in that vast and henceforth empty palace.

From early in the morning of October 5, driven to active protest by hunger and high prices, a huge crowd of women, accompanied too by men in women's clothes, had been gathering in the square outside the Hôtel de Ville. A trivial incident – an alleged insult to the revolutionary cockade at a banquet of the royal bodyguard three days before – had heightened suspicions of the King and court, and brought the discontents of weeks to a head. After invading the Hôtel de Ville, where they seized powder, guns and cannon, a crowd of some six thousand set out towards Versailles, demanding bread and the transfer of the government and royal family to Paris. They were followed some hours later by a section of the newly formed National Guard under the reluctant leadership of Lafayette; behind them came an indeterminate rabble, armed with muskets, pikes and scythes, almost certainly incited by the Duc d'Orléans who, with the hope of overthrowing the King and becoming Regent, had everything to gain by fomenting disorder.

At Versailles the National Assembly was in session while the King had gone out hunting. News of the approach of the mob, who were making the twelve mile journey from Paris through a day of wind and rain, reached Versailles about noon. The King was recalled from hunting, the Queen from the gardens of the Petit Trianon to the palace where a hastily assembled council debated what was to be done. The King as usual was indecisive. It was against his inclination to flee, against his principles to fire on a crowd composed largely of women. It was decided in the end to barricade the palace – the great grilles were drawn across the entrance to the courtyard for the first time in a century – but not to take up arms against the mob.

Madame de Staël had been in Paris when she heard the news of the march. Hastening to join her parents in Versailles, she arrived there by a little used route in mid-afternoon. Her father was locked in conference with the King, her mother, painfully agitated but determined to share her husband's fate, was among the crowd of courtiers gathered anxiously outside the royal apartments. In an atmosphere of mounting apprehension they awaited the arrival of the marchers.

"Night approached," wrote Madame de Staël, "and our fears were growing with the darkness when we saw M. de Chinon (later Duc de Richelieu) . . . arriving at the palace. He was pale and exhausted and he wore the clothes of a common man; it was the first time such a dress had been seen in the residence of kings. . . . He had been marching for some distance with the crowd in order to overhear what was being said and had then left it in order to reach Versailles and warn the royal family. What a story he told! Women and children armed with pikes and scythes, gathered from all parts. The dregs of the population brutalised by drink and rags. In the midst of this hellish crowd men nicknamed *coupe-têtes* and determined to deserve the title."

Drenched, hungry and exhausted, after a six hour journey in the pouring rain, the women of the mob seemed as much to be pitied as feared when at last they straggled into Versailles. Their first stop was the National Assembly where, having harangued the deputies and occupied the President's chair, they settled down for a long and noisy night's session. Meanwhile, in the squares and avenues outside the palace a crowd some thousands strong had congregated. Fires were lit, a horse which had been killed was cooked and eaten, women mingled with the soldiers set to guard the palace gates. Some – chief among them, according to tradition, Théroigne de Méricourt – were seen distributing money in order to subvert them: the money, it was hinted, came from the coffers of the Duc d'Orléans.

Carlyle had pictured Théroigne de Méricourt – "brown locked

Théroigne" – astride a cannon at the head of the mob leaving Paris. Michelet showed her among the soldiers at Versailles "with her feathered hat and scarlet riding habit, a sabre by her side, her words tumbling out pell mell, half in Flemish, half in French . . . impetuous, charming, terrible". Her own account was more prosaic. Already based in Versailles, where she had moved to be close to the National Assembly, she had confined her activities to wandering among the crowd. "People were speaking against the aristocrats," she wrote. "I joined in too, and that in no uncertain terms."

Inside the palace, now virtually in a state of siege, all hopes were pinned on the arrival of Lafayette who with fifteen thousand soldiers of the National Guard was expected within the next few hours. Having failed to organise the King and royal family's escape, his ministers stood dejectedly and in silence, a prey to the gloomiest forebodings. "Silently too," wrote Madame de la Tour du Pin, "people walked up and down that gallery which had seen all the splendours of the monarchy since the days of Louis XIV. The Queen remained in her room with Madame Elizabeth and Madame. The card room, which was almost in darkness, was filled with women who spoke in whispers, some sitting on tabourets, others on the tables. As for myself, I was so agitated that I could not remain still a moment . . . the waiting seemed unbearable."

It was just after midnight when the glow of distant torches announced the approach of Lafayette and the National Guard. Fatigue, the rain and the late hour had already quietened the crowd, now seeking shelter in stables and outhouses around the palace or moving to the wineshops of the town. At five in the morning, having made his dispositions to defend the palace, Lafayette retired for that famous hour of sleep that would earn him the title of General Morpheus, the "man who slept against his King".

Madame de la Tour du Pin, unwilling to return to her father-in-law's apartments at the War Ministry, where a mob of women had invaded the kitchens and ante-rooms, was sleeping in her aunt's apartments in the palace. She was wakened by the sound of shouts outside. "I shook myself," she wrote, "for I had been very fast asleep, and then climbed onto the window and leaned out over the leads. But they jutted out too far for me to be able to see the streets. I could distinctly hear a number of voices shouting 'Kill them! Kill them! Kill the Gardes du Corps!'"

A few minutes later her terrified maid arrived from the Ministry. On her way she had encountered a mob of people, and seen one in the act of beheading the body of a member of the Gardes du Corps who had just been killed. Realising that her clean gown and white apron made her dangerously conspicuous, she had fled at once, stepping over the body of another guard who had fallen across the gate of the Cour Royale as she did so.

She had scarcely completed her dramatic story than La Tour du Pin arrived and in a few words was able to tell them what had happened — the door left open, the storming of the marble staircase, the Queen's desperate escape to the King's bedchamber while the mob battered at the doors of the ante-chamber to her own. Insisting that it was dangerous to remain so close to the royal apartments, he persuaded his unwilling wife to move to a friend's house near the Orangerie, while he himself returned to duty with the King.

Madame de Staël, like Madame de la Tour du Pin, had had a rude awakening. "A very old woman, the mother of the Comte de Choiseul Gouffier . . . rushed into my bedroom; she came in terror, seeking refuge, although I did not enjoy the honour of her acquaintance." On hearing her news and terrified that Necker, who had already left for the palace, might be in danger, Madame de Staël and her mother set out to follow him down the long passages that led from the Contrôle Général to the royal apartments. As they approached they heard shots being fired in the courtyard and when they reached the long gallery saw splashes of blood on the floor. But they arrived when the worst was over. Lafayette, hastily aroused, had immediately rallied the National Guard to come to the aid of the hard pressed Gardes du Corps, who having now routed their attackers, were embracing their rescuers with cries of "*Vive Lafayette!*"

From the courtyard outside the crowd had been clamouring for the transfer of the King and royal family to Paris. Their assent had just been given and the shots that they had heard had been fired in jubilation. The Queen then entered the salon. Her hair was in disorder, wrote Madame de Staël, her face was pale but dignified, her whole bearing struck the imagination unforgettably. The mob was calling for her to appear on the balcony; the whole courtyard below, the Cour de Marbre, was filled with armed men and it was plain from her face what she feared. She walked forward nonetheless without hesitating, and Madame de Staël, recalling the scene, reflected on the fickleness of the mob, who having wished, perhaps, to kill her only hours before, now acclaimed her to the skies.

When she left the balcony the Queen went up to Madame Necker and said in a voice choked with sobs: "They want to compel the King and me to go to Paris with the heads of our bodyguards carried before us on pikes."

"This was exactly what happened," wrote Madame de Staël. "Thus were the King and Queen conducted to Paris. We ourselves [the Neckers] returned by another way, far from this terrible spectacle. Our path led through the Bois de Boulogne. Scarcely a leaf was stirring, the landscape, bathed in sunlight, seemed to mock at our distress."

La tour du Pin, at the King's request, remained behind with his regiment to guard the palace. "A frightful solitude already reigned over Versailles," wrote Madame de la Tour du Pin. "No other sound could be heard in the palace but that of gates, doors and shutters which had not been closed since the time of Louis XIV." Fearful of further disorders, her husband refused to let her stay by his side, and towards evening, with her aunt and a maid, she made her melancholy departure from the palace and a way of life she would never know again.

Chapter 3

The march of the women on Versailles, like the storming of the Bastille, was one of the great symbolic events of the French Revolution, immense in its effects on the European imagination. The image of the women of Paris, armed with pikes, riding cannons, fixed itself in the iconography of the period. It was an image that would do no service to the cause of women's rights, helping to cast them, when the reaction to the Revolution came, as dangerous and de-natured, and hence unfit to play a part in politics.

For the real significance of the march was political – it was part of the process of democratisation which, since the fall of the Bastille, had spread down through every level of the population. The people, "*le peuple*", were discovering both their political identity and their powers. Democracy begins with numbers: the women who helped to swell the mob in the attack on the Bastille, and who dominated the march on Versailles, were a vital element in the first great crowd scenes of the Revolution.

Nor was the march an isolated event. From July 14 on there had been a series of processions by the women of the town in thanksgiving for the fall of the Bastille. *Le Moniteur* of August 9, for instance, reported a procession of the women of Les Halles:

"Escorted with brilliant music and accompanied by a detachment of the National Guard whose arms were ornamented with flowers and ribbons, followed by a crowd of young persons dressed in white, [they] marched with pomp to the church of Sainte Geneviève, patron saint of Paris. A solemn mass was celebrated, followed by a *Te Deum*, to thank heaven for the happy revolution which had just taken place."

The march to Versailles had stemmed in part from this tradition, and the returning journey, for all the bloodshed that preceded it, had also something of a festive feeling, the women carrying branches of green foliage, and many of them decked from head to foot with tricolour cockades.

For the hapless passengers in the royal coach this festive feeling was hardly uppermost. They had narrowly escaped being massacred, they knew themselves to be the prisoners of the mob. When Madame de Staël the next day attended the Queen's reception for the court and diplomatic corps at the Tuileries Palace, dusty and dilapidated after a century of disuse, the Queen was unable to pronounce a word, so suffocating were her sobs. The guests too, wrote Madame de Staël, found it impossible to speak.

With the arrival of the royal family in Paris a temporary lull seemed to have been reached in public affairs. In less than five months, it could be claimed, the main objectives of the Revolution had been achieved. Feudalism had been abolished, the rights of man had been declared, the King was in the midst of his people. The Constituent Assembly, as the National Assembly was known, was embarked on the work of framing France's constitution. The year that followed, a year of sweeping reconstruction and reform, would be known as *l'année heureuse*.

Never had the salons of Paris been more involved in the discussion of France's destiny. "Conversation in society," wrote Madame de Staël to the King of Sweden, with whom since her marriage she had been in regular correspondence, "is no longer unprofitable since public opinion is formed and made in that way. Words have become actions." Her salon at the Swedish embassy in the rue du Bac was a forum for liberal – but not radical – opinion. On Tuesday evenings she could be seen at the centre of her mother's gatherings at the Treasury, now moved with the rest of the administration to Paris. Stiff and prudish – "God after creating her dipped her in starch" – Madame Necker received rather than welcomed her guests. Her daughter's intimate supper parties on Thursday evenings, when twelve or fifteen guests would gather by candlelight in the little salon, *la chambre ardente*, had a very different atmosphere. Political discussions, play readings, rehearsals of speeches for the next day's National Assembly would continue late into the night. Necker, discreet and ponderous, could be seen in conversation with Talleyrand, "who smiled in order not to speak and spoke in order not to answer". Narbonne, in close attendance on Madame de Staël, allowed himself to be chaffed on her friendship for Talleyrand – the line between love and friendship was never one she clearly drew – but in the eyes of Gouverneur Morris at least showed signs of jealousy. Freshly arrived and with no axe to grind, Governeur Morris gives precious glimpses of these evenings. At first he was conscious of his New World awkwardness – "I feel very stupid in this company," he confessed to his diary – but the feeling had soon worn off. From Madame de Staël he received "not exactly what Falstaff calls 'a leer of promise' but what amounts to the same thing", but neither he nor she took matters any further. He listened instead to the complaints of her husband, increasingly unhappy at his wife's infidelities, and he was quick to notice her Achilles heel: "I have never before met anything like her extravagant vanity on behalf of her father," he wrote.

If Madame de Staël's salon, dedicated to Necker's glory, was a powerful political centre, it was only one of many. The salons of the hard line aristocracy were dwindling – emigration had already taken its toll of many of its greatest names. But those of the liberals abounded. In the rue de Tournon the Comtesse de Beauharnais, ripe in age but as irresistibly feminine as Madame de Staël was virile, presided over evenings where "equality and liberty were her trump cards". It was a salon where the spirit of Voltaire still reigned and where the young man of the house was Alexandre de Beauharnais, a future president of the National Assembly. His Creole wife, the seductive Joséphine,* was not present at these gatherings. Having borne him two children, she had recently

---

*Then known by her Christian names of Marie-Josèphe-Rose; it was Napoleon who first called her Joséphine.

obtained a legal separation and returned to her native Martinique. Husband and wife would only be reconciled in the shadow of the guillotine.

Elsewhere, in the Palais de la Monnaie, the high-minded Marquise de Condorcet, twenty years younger than her philosopher husband, held sway in a salon whose tone was severely intellectual and whose politics were well to the left of Madame de Staël's. More pleasure loving was the group surrounding the young Marquise de Fontaney, who would take her place in history as Madame Tallien. The daughter of the powerful Spanish banker Cabarrus, she had created a sensation when she arrived in Paris three years earlier at the age of just fifteen. "No lovelier creature," wrote Madame de la Tour du Pin, "ever emerged from the hands of the creator." Now married, but leading a separate existence from her husband, she had flung herself into the Revolution as she would have thrown herself into any new fashion – her salon was thronged with admirers of all parties.

The Revolution was the fashion. The Queen's dressmaker, Rose Bertin, had lost her aristocratic customers, the great hooped skirts and powdered hair of the past had given place to modest muslins and cottons, to hair caught back in loosely hanging curls or cut short in the Grecian manner. The tricolour was everywhere, in cockades, flowers and ribbons; dresses of Indian cotton were printed with bouquets in red, white and blue, or broadly striped in the three colours; blue jackets would be trimmed with high red collars braided in white. Names of colours reflected political enthusiasms: a certain blue (for the King was still popular) was known as *bleu de roi*, a shade of scarlet by the sinister name of *sang de Foulon* (the luckless minister hacked to pieces by the mob). Elaborate or expensive jewellery was no longer acceptable – in December 1789 Necker had opened the Caisse Patriotique, great ladies had thrown in their jewellery, their enamelled patch boxes, their paste and silver buckles. The most elegant jewellery that could be worn was something associated with the fall of the Bastille. Madame de Genlis, the former mistress of the Duc d'Orléans, and still, it was said, his *éminence grise*, wore a polished piece of stone from the ruins of the Bastille, surrounded by laurel leaves and pinned on a positive forest of tricolour ribbons.

★　★　★

The salons of the liberal aristocracy were open to men from other ranks of society, politicians, journalists and men of letters. They were far less open to women. Théroigne de Méricourt would have no hope of being received in an aristocratic salon, and it is interesting to note that despite her democratic convictions she herself had sought to raise her status by adding an aristocratic "de" to her name and indeed passing for a time under the assumed name of the Comtesse de Campinado. It was an aspiration that reflected the realities of life in pre-revolutionary France. Even Robespierre had set store by the "de" to his name, and Madame Roland, later the Egeria of the Girondins, had spent long months intriguing to get her husband's patents of nobility admitted.

At the noisy sessions of the National Assembly, now gathered in the Manège, a former riding school close to the Tuileries, Théroigne de Méricourt had become a familiar figure. The first to arrive in the morning and the last to leave, it was she, according to contemporaries, who habitually gave the signal for the chorus of applause or dissent which punctuated the debates. Strikingly dressed, sometimes in the famous scarlet riding habit in which she was pictured in the October days, sometimes in Grecian garb, she rapidly attracted notice. She founded a club, "*Les Amis de la Loi*", which drew in the celebrities of the Left. She proposed patriotic motions, for example the presentation of cockades and civic crowns to deserving deputies. But her finest moment came when towards the end of February 1790 she made an appearance at the Club des Cordeliers. It was described by Camille Desmoulins in his newly founded paper *Les Révolutions de France et de Brabant*:

"I was about to retire," he wrote, " . . . when the usher

23

announced to the president that a young woman demanded to enter the Senate. It was the celebrated Mademoiselle Théroigne, who had come to ask to take the floor and to propose a motion. She was unanimously admitted to the bar. One member, overcome with enthusiasm on seeing her, exclaimed: 'It is the Queen of Sheba, come to see the Solomon of the Districts.' 'Yes,' replied Mademoiselle Théroigne, taking her cue from the words with great aplomb, 'it is the fame of your wisdom which has brought me to your midst. Prove that you are indeed Solomon, that it is your prerogative to build the Temple, and that you will lose no time in building the Temple of the National Assembly.'"

Her proposal – to build a Temple of Liberty on the foundations of the Bastille – was received, wrote Camille, with a "fury of applause" and the assembly voted her the honours of the session.

Far different was her image in the royalist press in whose scurrilous and witty pages she featured regularly as the "lover of the nation", offering her favours indiscriminately to all the leading figures of the left. Her special favourite, supposedly, was the left wing deputy Marie-Etienne Populus, his surname doubling for the 'populus' or people, to all of whom, thanks to her democratic sympathies, she was said to be available. In one particularly offensive scene she is shown in childbirth in the National Assembly, rolling in convulsions on the President's table as she is delivered of the *embryon national*. All the deputies in turn dispute the baby's parentage – its malformed foot recalls Talleyrand (who limped from a childhood injury), its bellowing voice that of Mirabeau, its ravishing backside the great Populus himself. The prodigious child then raises itself, growing larger by the second, and speaks: "You all of you dispute the honour of having fathered me," he declares, "and all of you have made a contribution. I swear it by the civic virtues of my mother."

These kind of attacks, in papers of both left and right, were nothing unusual. Madame de Staël and the Queen, to name only two, were constantly depicted in the crudest terms. But, while both occupied great positions, Théroigne de Méricourt's curious fame rested on little more than her enthusiastic and exhibitionist appearances at the National Assembly. Her celebrity snowballed, and with it her legend. It was only at the beginning of 1790, by which time she was appearing regularly in the press, that she was described as having taken part in the storming of the Bastille. More alarmingly in the official enquiries which were opened into the events of October 5–6, she began to be mentioned as one of the leading figures in the women's march. Before long the story that she had tried to bribe the troops, and even planned the assassination of the Queen, had taken hold. In May 1790, feeling seriously menaced by the enquiries, she withdrew to her native Liège. Her reputation followed her however. Police spies kept watch on her movements, and she was soon reported stirring up revolution among her fellow countrymen.

★　★　★

The Fête de la Fédération, on July 14, 1790, was the high moment of *l'année heureuse*, the crowning, as it seemed, of the Revolution's triumph. Madame de Staël catches the euphoria of the times. "Despite its faults," she wrote, "the Constituent Assembly had brought about so many benefits and triumphed over so many evils that it was adored by almost all of France. . . One breathed more freely, there was more air in one's lungs, and the indefinite hope of a happiness without bounds had taken hold of the nation in all its force."

It was in this spirit that preparations for the celebrations of the anniversary of the fall of the Bastille in Paris took place. Delegates of the National Guard were expected from every department in France, the vast expanse of the Champ de Mars was to be transformed into a colossal amphitheatre. Since it was clearly impossible that the work of levelling it, and raising a terraced ramp of earth around it to accommodate the spectators, could be finished in time by the ten thousand labourers working on it, the whole population of Paris took a hand in the work. "Such an extraordinary spectacle will never be seen again," wrote Madame de la Tour du Pin, whose husband had been given the task of arranging the accommodation for the many deputations. "Thousands of barrows were pushed by people of every quality. In Paris, there were still some monasteries where the monks continued to wear their habits, and you could see Capuchin monks and friars pulling beside the ladies of the town, clearly recognisable by their dress, both harnessed to small tip carts known as 'camions'. Laundresses and Knights of Saint Louis worked side by side in that great gathering of all the people; there was not the slightest disorder or the smallest dispute. Everyone was moved by the same impulse: fellowship."

The day of the Fête de la Fédération was a rainy one, but nothing dampened the enthusiasm of the vast crowd, nor of the thirty thousand delegates from the army, the navy and the National Guard, whose brightly coloured uniforms vied with the rainbow hues of the umbrellas sheltering the audience. At an altar in the centre Talleyrand, whose famous resolution transferring the Church's property to the State was still in the process of being enacted, celebrated mass in full episcopal splendour, assisted by three hundred priests in tricolour sashes. At a platform at one end sat the King and royal family with all the court. The Queen, noted Madame de la Tour du Pin, was making a tremendous effort to hide her ill humour at the occasion, but was not succeeding very well.

Madame de Staël, with an eye on her father, saw that his face too was gloomy and distraught. At the height of the nation's joy and the seeming union between King and people, the limited monarchy for which he had worked, he knew himself to be almost at the end of his resources. Increasingly ignored by the National Assembly, despised by Mirabeau, who christened him "the clock that always runs slow", he had sacrificed his popularity in his attempts to follow a moderate course. Less than six weeks later he would be forced to resign. He retired to Coppet, his château in Switzerland, narrowly escaping arrest on the way. Madame de Staël, who had just given birth to a baby of whom Narbonne was probably the father, remained behind in Paris for another month. In early October, her first political illusions shattered, she set out to join his exile.

Chapter 4

In the wave of patriotic emotion which swept France in 1789 and 1790 there were few who espoused the cause of liberty more ardently than Manon Roland, wife of an inspector of manufactures in Lyon, who two years later would spring to prominence as Minister of the Interior. The daughter of a Parisian engraver, self-educated, intelligent and energetic, she had long chafed at the indignities of her petit-bourgeois station. A visit to Versailles as a young woman, when she had stayed in the servants' quarters under the eaves of the palace, had confirmed a lasting hatred of the aristocracy and more particularly of the Queen. The fact that she had married above herself – her husband's family had pretensions to the nobility – had done nothing to efface her early impressions. The advent of the Revolution saw all her hopes and aspirations come to life. "Friends of humanity, lovers of liberty," she wrote, "we believed that it would regenerate the race. . . . We welcomed it with rapture."

In the years before the Revolution she had collected round her a circle of respectful admirers, idealists and radical thinkers like herself. With a husband twenty years older, she prided herself on a positively Roman virtue, taking pleasure in displaying herself as an ideal wife and mother before an audience of younger men. Her husband, industrious, tetchy and pedantic, took part in these friendships, but it was his wife who was the guiding spirit. She was thirty-five years old, fresh faced, full figured, with loosely curling dark hair, strong white teeth and an abundance of good health. A lonely and not always happy youth had given her great tracts of time for study. She was widely read in English and Italian, steeped in the theories of Rousseau and, like so many of her contemporaries, a passionate admirer of the Greek and Roman past. After a fervent Catholic childhood she had rejected the doctrines of the Church. "I'm still in the balance of doubt," she wrote, "and rest there peacefully suspended, like an Indian in his hammock." But she remained as fervent as any *dévote* in the principles she imposed upon herself, hard work, self-discipline, above all fidelity to her husband.

From the first her marriage had been less than rapturous. It was a "severe bond", she wrote, in which the woman took responsibility for the happiness of both. She sublimated any discontents in the upbringing of her daughter Eudora (though the child proved disappointingly dull and unresponsive), in the duties of her household, and in her husband's work. His numerous monographs on scientific and economic subjects, his three volume *Dictionary of Manufactures*, his articles on politics, all bore the stamp of his wife's hand. Unlike Madame de Staël, who from an early age had sought literary glory, Madame Roland was content to remain anonymous. It was not a woman's place, she thought, to venture into authorship, though with the outset of the Revolution she allowed extracts from her letters to a lawyer, Jacques Pierre Brissot, with whom she and her husband were in correspondence, to be published in his Paris newsheet *Le Patriote Français*. Printed under the by-line "Letters from a Roman lady", they appeared with flattering frequency, while another, this time anonymous, article on the patriotic celebrations in the Champ de la Fédération in Lyon, was reprinted in full in Camille Desmoulins' *Révolutions de France et de Brabant*.

But Lyon, for all its industrial and mercantile importance, was a town on the periphery of events. It was Paris that was the magnet for those with political ambitions and a desire to be at the centre of things. So it was with joy that she learned, towards the beginning of 1791, that her husband had been appointed by the municipality of Lyons to negotiate the payment of the city's debts in Paris. They arrived there on February 20, 1791, leaving the nine year old Eudora in a convent school in Lyon, and set up house on the left bank. Before long they had gathered round them a circle which included not only former friends but such figures of the left as Robespierre, Pétion (later mayor of Paris), and Brissot, till then only known from correspondence, but emerging already as leader of that radical group who would later take the name of Brissotins or, as they were better known, Girondins.* The form of government sought by Madame de Staël and the liberal constitutionalists – a limited monarchy along British lines – was one that already seemed too tame to Madame Roland and her friends. Inspired by the stern republican heroes of Plutarch, and finding parallels for themselves among them – Madame Roland had taken to calling her husband Cato – their ideal was a republic, not a constitutional monarchy. With a bluntness even her apologists find excessive, Madame Roland had denounced the royal family as early as the summer of 1789. "If the National Assembly fails to put these two crowned heads on trial, or some generous Decius does not strike them down, you are all *foutus*."

But the time for such opinions was not ripe. Meanwhile she absorbed herself in the spectacle of public affairs. She joined the noisy crowds that thronged the gardens of the Palais Royal. She attended the meetings of the Society of Friends of the Constitution, otherwise known as the Jacobins. She followed the sessions of the Constituent Assembly, shocked at the slowness and disorder of the proceedings, consumed with hatred for the royalists or "blacks". In the evenings, in their small apartment, she presided over meetings of her husband's friends. Not for her the luxuries and sophistication of the aristocratic salons which she despised. Sugared water was the usual drink, with sometimes a simple meal which she prepared herself. Nor did she seek to shine in general conversation. While the circle of men discussed the issues of the day she sat a little way removed from them, ostensibly sewing or writing letters, but missing not a word. She never spoke, though often, as she admitted, she had to bite her lip not to do so.

Her memoirs give pictures of their visitors: Brissot, living in honourable poverty, austere in principle but regrettably light

*So called, because a number of its leading members came from the *département* of the Gironde in South West France.

minded as a character; Robespierre, cool, sarcastic, speaking little at their meetings, but creaming off the ideas of others to use at the Jacobins thereafter; the serious and idealistic young Buzot, whom she had already singled out as exceptional and for whom she would one day have a softer feeling.

Fresh faced and open, radiant with energy and enthusiasm, Madame Roland exercised a powerful attraction on those around her. Roland, grey haired and dessicated, seemed more like her father than her husband. Friends compared them to a Quaker and his daughter – Madame Roland always cultivated simplicity in dress. But simplicity in any case was the fashion and her dresses, modestly sprigged or striped, with muslin fichus round the neck and shoulders, went well with her wholesome good looks.

The hopes of the moderates in the previous year – that the Constituent Assembly would achieve the Revolution's aims – were foundering in 1791. The sudden death of Mirabeau in April had removed a vital link between the court and the Assembly; from then on the gap could only widen. It was the King who was the stumbling block. He had allowed the nationalisation of the church's lands against his conscience, but with the Pope's denunciation of the civil oath imposed upon the clergy he reached his sticking point. Still publicly maintaining his loyalty to the Revolution, he was privately planning his escape from Paris. On June 20 came the flight to Varennes: his ignominious capture and return dealt a shattering blow to the confidence of those who felt that King and Constitution could work together. From then on, whatever legal fictions were put forward to cover the facts, the King was a prisoner in the Tuileries.

Madame Roland was outspoken in her reaction to the royal flight: "The King has reached the lowest stage of vileness; he has been shown up nakedly by those around him; he inspires nothing but scorn. . . . People call him Louis the False, or the fat pig. . . . It is impossible to envisage a being so totally despised on the throne."

Her violent views, however, were not yet shared by Assembly. Though Robespierre spoke out strongly against the King and the word republic was openly mentioned, the majority of deputies were still not psychologically prepared to overthrow him. The King was temporarily suspended while the forces of the moderate Right did their best to rally to his support. Breaking away from the Jacobin Club, they formed a new association of their own in the Convent of the Feuillants, the name by which they would henceforth be known. And on July 17, over-reacting to the fear of a riot, the National Guard under Lafayette opened fire on a crowd that had gathered in the Champ de Mars to call for the abdication of the King. They left behind them more than fifty dead.

The massacre of the Champ de Mars and the fear of right wing reprisals sent the Left into temporary disarray. Robespierre went into hiding – Madame Roland, then one of his greatest admirers, had sent round to offer him a refuge in their home, but he had already found a hiding place elsewhere. Marat sought safety in the sewers, his bloodthirsty paper *L'Ami du Peuple* for the time being closed down. Camille Desmoulins ceased publishing his *Révolutions de France et de Brabant*. The Rolands, disgusted at the turn things had taken, and Roland's mission in Paris virtually completed, returned to Lyon and their country estate nearby.

★ ★ ★

For all her passionate involvement in politics Madame Roland had never sought to play a direct role in public affairs. Deliberately self-effacing in company – though outspoken in private – she consistently paid lip service to the idea of masculine superiority. "It often angers me," she wrote, "to see women disputing privileges which ill befit them. . . . However gifted they may be in some respects they should never show their talents or learning in public." At no time in her career, either as the influential hostess of 1791, or later as the wife of a minister, did she seek to associate herself with the tide of women's aspirations to which the Revolution gave rise.

Though women in general had enjoyed no political rights under the *ancien régime* a few had been able to exercise electoral privileges in the election of the States General – groups of women in religious orders, and noblewomen who either as widows, or by some anomaly, enjoyed feudal rights. The abolition of religious orders, and the ending of feudal rights, had done away with these exceptions. At the very moment that the *Declaration of the Rights of Man* declared all men to be created equal, women, for the first time, found themselves with no political rights at all.

In the early stages of the Revolution, when through their presence in its great crowd scenes, women had played a major role, the idea of specific political rights for women was not an important issue. For the vast majority of women, conditioned to accept the *status quo*, it would never become so. Among the educated classes, the influence of Rousseau, with his glorification of motherhood, was strong. It coloured the debates on education in the National Assembly. Though a few lone voices called for equal opportunities for girls in education, most shared the view, expressed at its most extreme by Prudhomme, the editor of the *Révolutions de Paris*, "Does the mother of a family need books to bring up children? Has she not the book of nature and her heart?"

The argument was carried through to women's rights. "The common good, above all that of women," wrote Talleyrand in a report to the Constituent Assembly, "demands that they do not aspire to the exercise of political rights and functions. Let us seek their interests in the wish of nature. Is it not apparent that their delicate constitutions, their gentle dispositions, the numerous duties of maternity, must always distance them from powerful commitments and strenuous duties, and call them to peaceful occupations and household cares?"

This picture, generally accepted, of women as beings too delicate to enter the hurly burly of public life was a convenient fiction to cover the realities of their situation. Reforms improving women's private lot would be forthcoming: an equal share in family inheritances, the right to act as witnesses in legal matters, eventually divorce. But they remained economically dependent, legally minors, denied employment except in a few specific trades – a major area of employment, the lace industry, collapsed with the departure of the aristocracy and the changes in fashion brought about by the Revolution. Though a number of women, in *cahiers des doléances,*★ and in pamphlets and petitions thereafter had put forward specific complaints and demands, it was left not to a woman but a man to make the first major statement of the Revolution on their behalf.

The Marquis de Condorcet, heir to the great philosophical traditions of the eighteenth century, a disciple of Voltaire and Diderot, and a leading member of the Constituent Assembly, had long been an enemy to prejudice in every form. He had campaigned for civil rights for Protestants, for an end to slavery and the slave trade, and by a natural corollary for the civil rights of women. In the summer of 1790 he published his famous plea for women's suffrage, *Sur l'admission des femmes au droit de cité*. Already in an earlier work, *Lettre aux bourgeois de Newhaven*, he had taken as his starting point the rights of human kind in general: "Either no member of the human race has any natural rights or they all have the same; and anyone who votes against the rights of another, whatever their religion, their colour or their sex, has from that moment abjured his own."

In *Sur l'admission . . .*, published in the journal of the Society of 1789, an influential and eminently moderate body, he returned to the same theme. Long habit, he wrote, could so accustom human beings to the violation of their natural rights that they no longer missed or sought to claim them. "Is there any stronger proof of the power of habit, even among the enlightened, than to see the principle of equal rights invoked in the case of three or four hundred men, excluded through some absurd piece of prejudice, and to ignore the claims of twelve million women?"

He wittily dismissed the argument that women were biologically unfit to have the vote. "Why should people liable to pregnancies and passing indispositions not exercise rights of which one would not dream of depriving men who have gout each winter or catch cold easily?" Nor did he accept that women were intellectually inferior to men beyond the disadvantages of their education. (In his work on the Constitution two years later Condorcet consistently advocated equal education for boys and

★Lists of grievances presented to the States General.

girls.) Great women in history – Queen Elizabeth, Catherine the Great – had proved their capacity to govern. It was true that most women, by virtue of their role as wives and mothers, might find it hard to play a part in public life, but the same was true of the vast majority of working men. The government of a country would always be in the hands of a minority; it did not therefore follow that the majority should be denied the vote.

Condorcet's arguments, though much discussed in theory, had virtually no practical effect. Not only women's suffrage but the rights of men below a certain income level to vote were being questioned. With the electorate confined to so called "active" citizens – those who paid taxes of more than three days' wages every year the poorest members of society, like women at every level, were excluded from the vote. The only woman perhaps with an intellect or standing to match Condorcet's, Madame de Staël, held no brief for the other members of her sex. Intensely interested in power, she was content to exert it through the medium of the men she loved, her father first, Narbonne and others later. "It is right to exclude women from public affairs," she wrote. "Nothing is more opposed to their natural vocation than a relationship of rivalry with men, and personal celebrity will always bring the ruin of their happiness." However little she put her theories into practice, she felt no sense of female solidarity.

It was the less established women, on the fringes of society, who combined a passionate concern for the poor and underprivileged with one for their own sex. Théroigne de Méricourt was too eccentric, too exhibitionist and perhaps too little educated, to make a real impact on public opinion; in any case her views were seldom put on paper. But in 1791 a new figure in the saga of women's rights makes her entrance on the stage. A year before the publication of Mary Wollstonecraft's *A Vindication of the Rights of Women* in England, the playwright Olympe de Gouges published her manifesto, *The Rights of Woman*, in which echoing the clauses of the *Declaration of the Rights of Man* she demanded them for women too.

Olympe de Gouges, like Théroigne de Méricourt, had changed

her name and added a "de" to raise her status in the world of the ancien régime. Born Marie Gouze, the daughter of a butcher's wife in Languedoc, she claimed as her true father a local nobleman, the Marquis Le Franc de Pompignan. Though her claim was never recognised she maintained all her life the illusion of her noble birth, and among the many causes she espoused, that of bastards had a special place. Exceptionally beautiful when she was young, she had made her way through a series of amours – few other paths were open to a woman – to a life of affluence and extravagance. Now forty-four, her fine looks almost vanished, she continued to spend a fortune on clothes, on entertaining and on the horde of pets, from monkeys to a great dane, with which she was surrounded. Olympe de Gouges, amongst other fantasies, believed in the transmigration of souls; she saw her pets as former human beings, now serving out a time of expiation in the guise of animals; she christened them all by the names of past celebrities.

Fantasy, extravagance and feminine vanity were lifelong characteristics of Olympe de Gouges. They concealed a strong and original intelligence, and a zeal for justice which was fed by her own sense that she herself had been born to a destiny unworthy of her capacities. From her early career of gallantry she had turned to the world of letters. Through most of the 1780s she had been bombarding the Théâtre Français with her plays and having failed to have them staged, had published them with stinging prefaces denouncing actors, management and fellow playwrights. The only one to be performed, *L'Esclavage des Noirs*, a sentimental but deeply felt attack on slavery, was hissed off the stage after three performances – its theatrical failings apart, it is likely that it fell foul of the vested interests of the colonial lobby.

The coming of the Revolution gave a new impulse to her literary activities. The subject of her plays grew more political and she augmented them with a stream of pamphlets and brochures, proposing a wide variety of social measures – government workshops for the unemployed, a voluntary tax on wealth, improved conditions in maternity hospitals. Strongly opposed to all forms of unjust privilege, she remained a moderate in her political views, seeing in a constitutional monarchy the best hope for France. She admired Mirabeau who returned her admiration, writing gallantly, "Until now I had thought the graces adorned themselves only with flowers, but your thoughts are expressed with fluency and backed by intellectual power; your progress, like that of the Revolution, has been crowned with success."

Such compliments, however, were few and far between. As she bitterly observed: "I put forward a hundred propositions; they are received; but I am a woman; no one pays any attention." The fact that her pamphlets were hastily and carelessly written – she herself could barely spell – and mingled serious points with random reflections on her own concerns also helped to make it hard to take her seriously. Her pamphlet *The Rights of Woman*, which at the time aroused little more interest than the majority of her writings, combined in the same way a line of lucid and hard-hitting argument with an irrelevant complaint, in the final paragraphs, against a cab driver who had overcharged her. Two hundred years later, the cab driver, her plays, and her myriad other pamphlets forgotten, the *Rights of Woman* stands out as a prophetic document.

"O man," it began, "are you capable of justice? . . . By what sovereign right do you oppress my sex?" After a brief preamble, arguing that inequality between the sexes was contrary to the laws of nature, she moved to her central pronouncement. "The sex superior in beauty as in its courage in the course of maternal suffering," she wrote defiantly, "recognises and declares in the presence of the Supreme Being the following rights of Woman and the female Citizen." The paragraphs that followed, echoing those of the *Declaration of the Rights of Man* demanded equal rights with men before the law, in civic matters, in taxation and ownership of property. The idea of universal suffrage was implicit. "The law," she wrote in article VI, "must be the expression of the general will. All female and male citizens must contribute either personally or through their representatives in its formation; it must be the same for all; all female and male citizens, being equal in its eyes, must be equally admitted to all honours, positions and public employment according to their capacity and with no distinctions beyond those of their talents and their virtues." Freedom of speech was another fundamental. "No one," she wrote in article X, "must be disturbed for expressing their basic convictions; woman has the right to mount the scaffold; she has equally the right to mount the rostrum." It was a proposition which was soon to acquire a sinister resonance.

The pamphlet was dedicated to the Queen, whose influence she hoped would further women's rights – Olympe de Gouges was still a monarchist in sympathy. Its seventeen articles were followed by a general exhortation to her sex: "Women awake! The tocsin of enlightenment and reason resounds through the universe; recognise your rights." Whatever her feelings about men, Olympe de Gouges was far from approving the role of women in the past. "Women have been responsible for more harm than good. Constraint and dissimulation have been their lot. What they lost by force they gained by ruse, using all the resources of their charms. . . ." The Revolution had done away with women's nocturnal empire, the sex once "respected and despicable" had become "respectable and despised". It was time for them to claim their dues, to seek reforms in education and employment and to end their dependence on the whims of men. In marriage above all, which she saw as the "tomb of trust and love", a looser form of contract, with provision for the rights of natural children, was required. Her grudge against the Marquis Le Franc de Pompignan still rankled.

Hastily written – she prided herself on her speed in composition, which she saw as a product of her natural genius – Olympe de Gouges' pamphlet ended, as we have seen, with a complaint against her cab driver. A further paragraph was added, after the pamphlet had already gone to press, which reflected excitement on a very different level. The King, suspended from his duties since the flight to Varennes, had been re-instated. On September 14, 1791, he had formally accepted the Constitution. "I cannot prevent myself from stopping the press," she wrote, "to express the pure joy which fills my heart at the news that the King has accepted the Constitution. . . . Divine providence, grant that this public re-joicing may not be based on a false illusion!"

Chapter 5

With the King's acceptance of the new constitution, so joyfully greeted by Olympe de Gouges, the two years' work of the Constituent Assembly was completed. In the new Legislative Assembly, from which the former deputies of the Constituent Assembly were debarred, there was still a majority among the Constitutional monarchists or Feuillants. But they maintained an uneasy ascendancy. The menacing Treaty of Pillnitz (August 27), in which Austria and Prussia threatened armed intervention on the King's behalf, made war for the first time seem a possibility. In Paris the forces of the Left were regrouping. Fear of the mob, so brutally dispersed on the Champ de Mars, was ever present in the background.

For the time being, however, there was a resurgence of goodwill towards the monarchy. "The King and Queen," wrote Madame de Staël, "were urged to go to the opera; their entry was greeted with hearty cheers in which the whole audience joined. The ballet *Psyche* was being given. At the moment when the furies danced and waved their torches, filling the theatre with light, I saw the faces of the King and Queen lit up by this pale imitation of hell. A terrible foreboding overwhelmed me. . . . We strolled afterwards in the Champs Elysées, which was brilliantly lighted. . . . The King and Queen drove slowly through the crowd. The moment their carriage was recognised there were shouts of '*Vive le Roi*!' But these demonstrators were the same who had insulted this very king on his return from Varennes; their applause was of no more account than their abuse."

Incapable of keeping away from the centre of events, Madame de Staël had arrived in Paris from Switzerland in late August, leaving her baby in her disapproving parents' charge. Her return was greeted with pleasure by the gutter press, always pleased to have her as a target, and with ill concealed dismay by her husband. Since the flight to Varennes his position had become almost untenable. The King of Sweden, a firm upholder of monarchical principles, deplored the leftward turn of politics in France and the vociferous liberalism of his ambassador's wife. The tone of the embassy, he told de Staël, should be one of sadness and mourning, it should certainly not continue to be a centre of political intrigue.

Madame de Staël no longer had her father's interests to pursue in Paris. Morose and disappointed, he had retired to his château of Coppet near Geneva, there to devote his time to writing in defence of his period as Finance Minister. The first of these self justifications, *De l'administration de M. Necker par lui-même* had just appeared. His near arrest on his way from France to exile, when he had been accused of carrying off the nation's gold, had rankled in particular.

"As we walked together, my father and I," wrote Madame de Staël, "under the great trees of Coppet, which seemed to be friendly witnesses of his noble thoughts, he asked me once if I believed that the whole French nation had shared the vulgar suspicions of which he had been victim on his journey from Paris to Switzerland.

'It seems to me,' he said, 'that there were some districts where, until the very end, the purity of my aims and my devotion to France were recognised.'

"He had scarcely asked me this question before he brushed it aside as afraid of being too moved by my reply.

'Say no more,' he exclaimed. 'God can read my heart. That is enough.'"

Necker's day was over. It was on the shoulders of Narbonne, her lover, that Madame de Staël intended his mantle to fall. Regrouping her salon in her father's former mansion in the Chaussée d'Antin – since the embassy was no longer available – she set herself to intriguing on his behalf. The fact that Narbonne, for all his intelligence, was essentially a lightweight, did not deter her. "It needed nothing less than love, the great dreamer, the great fascinator of the world," wrote Michelet, "to make this passionate young woman imagine that one could put this young officer, this inconsistent *roué*, this light and glittering figure, at the head of so great a movement – that the immense sword of the Revolution could pass, as a gage of love, from a woman to a coxcomb."

It was the post of Foreign Minister, immensely important as Prussia and Austria seemed to be moving towards war, that Madame de Staël sought for her lover. He was not to obtain it, despite intensive lobbying, but in December 1791, by dint of incredible exertions by his mistress he was given the almost equally important nomination of Minister of War. "What glory for Madame de Staël," wrote the Queen sarcastically to Fersen, "what joy for her to have the whole army at her disposal."

* * *

Madame Roland, like Madame de Staël, had been chafing at being away from Paris. Whereas once she had written lyrically about the pastoral joys of the country, she now fretted at the nullity of provincial life. Her husband, whose republican views were anathema to the conservative establishment in Lyon, had failed to be elected as a member of the new Legislative Assembly. In late September, 1791, a decree abolishing inspectorships of manufactures put an end to his salary and his prospect of a pension after forty years. Their financial situation, even then, was not desperate; with a minor post in the Lyon administration, and his work on the *Dictionary of Manufactures*, there was enough for them to live on modestly. But, for Madame Roland, the abolition of his inspectorship was the signal for their return to Paris. He must go there, she insisted, to claim his pension, and to renew contact with the influential figures who might help him. Roland, who had been a reluctant wooer when they had married eleven years earlier, and who in their first years together had dominated the ménage, was now completely under his wife's thumb. Through their work together, he had come to depend on her support and judgement; he found it impossible to oppose her.

On December 15 they arrived once more in Paris, this time bringing their daughter with them, taking a cheap fourth-floor flat in the same building where they had formerly occupied more spacious lodgings on the first.

Back in Paris, Madame Roland found that the salon over which she had presided so graciously had more or less dissolved. Robespierre had always been cold in his manner to her; no longer a deputy, he was now a leading figure in the Jacobins, with little inclination for intimate gatherings. Pétion had become mayor of Paris, and his wife, when Madame Roland went to call, behaved so coolly to her that she vowed not to visit her again. Brissot, caught in the affairs of the Legislative Assembly, called less often. The high-minded Buzot had taken up an appointment as a judge in the provinces.

In this atmosphere, with money a problem, and her husband's claims showing little sign of prospering, Madame Roland's robust good health and spirits deserted her. She complained of tiredness and lack of energy, though the appointment of her husband as corresponding secretary of the Jacobin Club gave her at least a foot in politics, and a chance to share his work of answering letters to the club.

She was still in the doldrums when on March 23, 1792 their fortunes were dramatically and unexpectedly reversed. Narbonne had been dismissed. The Feuillant ministry had fallen. In the crisis that followed the initiative had passed to the Girondins or moderate Left. Since ministers could not be appointed from among the deputies the King had had to turn outside the Legislative Assembly to make his choice. Dumouriez, an able and dashing general, well in with both Girondins and Jacobins, was appointed Foreign Secretary, and given virtual *carte blanche* to choose the other ministers. The choice of Minister of the Interior fell on Roland, then totally unknown outside Girondin circles, but experienced in administration and impeccably "patriotic" in his views.

From a friend of Madame Roland's, Sophie Grandchamp, we

get a picture of her reception of the news. An intimate of the family, she had been a witness of Madame Roland's growing gloom, brought about, she felt, by frustration and the gnawing of unsatisfied ambition. Having been summoned round to see them on the morning after Dumouriez had called on Roland to offer him the post, she found both husband and wife still in bed after a sleepless night of indecision. Roland, more timid than his wife, balanced up the dangers and disadvantages that such responsibilities would bring. Madame Roland, though greatly agitated, had persuaded him to accept.

The change in their position called, inevitably, for a change of setting. While they prepared to move to their official residence, the obliging Sophie Grandchamp arranged with their landlady that the first floor apartment should be made available. Having spent the day on errands for her friends she returned there late that evening to find a very different scene. Madame Roland, half dead that morning, had recovered all her grace and freshness. The room was filled with deputies and ministers, all singing her praises and those of her husband who appeared well pleased to hear them. Two footmen stood at the door to let in the guests. Poor Madame Grandchamp, quite unnoticed, flung herself down in a chair beside the fire and reflected on the mutability of fortune.

★ ★ ★

Narbonne's loss of office as Minister of War had indirectly been Roland's gain. "A man of wit," as Gouverneur Morris put it, but "by no means a man of business," he had held the post for less than three months; his dismissal would sound the death knell for the monarchists in France.

Narbonne had begun his ministry in a whirl of energy. Genuinely enthusiastic, he had set off almost immediately on an inspection of France's armies and defences, travelling day and night on a tour of the country's north and eastern frontiers. What he saw was discouraging. The army's numbers were under strength, morale was low, discipline was undermined, not least by the loss of

43

many officers who, as aristocrats, had departed to join the armed companies of émigrés now massing on the frontiers. He set improvements under way, and harried the National Assembly for money and recruits; at the same time, as the threat of hostilities loomed closer, he despatched Talleyrand to England on a mission to ensure her neutrality in the event of war. In all this Madame de Staël was his chief publicist and supporter. "The activities of Madame de St . . . for her beloved Narbonne are unbelievable," wrote a royalist paper; " . . . from nine in the morning she can be seen running to the journalists in her petticoat and bodice to communicate the official announcements, reports and letters which she dictates to her dear lover."

In early January, Madame de Staël's husband, recalled to Stockholm by the King of Sweden, had left Paris, having failed "despite every argument of tenderness and reason" to persuade her to accompany him. The Swedish embassy in the rue du Bac once more became her headquarters, a focus for the politics of the Centre which in the face of increasing polarisation to left and right she consistently sought to promote. The idea of a constitutional monarchy was proving even harder to sustain. Neither the King, secretly hoping that the Constitution of 1791 would prove unworkable, nor the Jacobins who sought his overthrow, had any interest in pursuing it.

Narbonne, perhaps, was the man best suited to rally a party of the Centre. In the National Assembly he had the support of the Feuillants and to some extent of the Girondins. But he was detested by the Jacobins of the extreme Left, and distrusted by the King. Louis XVI, who had appointed him only under pressure, had never thought him suitable to be a minister. In this he was seconded by the Queen, whose dislike of Madame de Staël, and hence her lover, was only equalled by her earlier dislike of Necker. Narbonne's attempts to persuade the King that his salvation lay in wholehearted support of the Constitution, and in strengthening the Centre, were doomed to failure.

Meanwhile the country was moving towards war, with almost every shade of opinion except for the extreme Left, in favour of it.

For the Girondins it would confirm the country's commitment to the Revolution and carry its ideas across Europe; for the royalists it was a chance to regain control of the situation with Austria and Prussia's help. The Feuillants, unwilling to enter into a major conflict, saw advantages in a brief campaign, from which a victorious army could return to re-establish law and order. Narbonne, while accepting this argument, had no illusions about its dangers. "War seems to me inevitable," he wrote, " . . . everything seems to be hurrying towards collapse, public distrust [of the King] is at its height, and this war, which we have so many good reasons to fear, is perhaps the only shadow of hope which is left."

His own period as a minister was coming to an end. Opposed at court, attacked by the Left, he lacked a solid base amidst the shifting loyalties of the National Assembly. Unable to carry through the measures he wished to strengthen the country's defences, he offered to resign. Madame de Staël, with perhaps excessive zeal, orchestrated simultaneous protests from Lafayette and his fellow generals; Narbonne, with a tactlessness verging on defiance, arranged for the letters to be published. It was too much for the King. Exasperated, he dismissed Narbonne. His departure was the signal for an outcry in the National Assembly, and the moment for the Girondins to establish their own claims. Less than a fortnight later the Feuillant ministry was replaced by a ministry dominated by the Gironde.

On April 20, three weeks after the Girondins had come to power, the King, flanked by his new ministers, appeared in the National Assembly to propose the declaration of war.

"On entering the Assembly," wrote Madame de Staël, "he looked to left and right with that sort of vacant curiosity one finds in people who are so short sighted they can hardly see. He proposed war in the same tone of voice with which he would have proposed the least important measure in the world."

The Assembly, in contrast, voted for the war with wild enthusiasm:

"The deputies threw their hats in the air, and that day, the first of that bloody conflict which would tear Europe apart for twenty-three years, was greeted by almost all without the slightest shadow of anxiety. Nonetheless, among the deputies who voted for that war, a great number were to perish violently, and those who rejoiced the most, unknown to themselves, had just pronounced their death sentence."

Chapter 6

Early in February 1792 a striking figure in a scarlet riding habit, with a feathered hat, and a mass of tumbling brown curls, had mounted the rostrum of the Jacobin Club in the rue Saint-Honoré. It was, of course, Théroigne de Méricourt. She had returned to Paris a few weeks earlier after ten months of dramatic and picturesque adventure. In March 1791 she had been kidnapped from her native Liège by two fanatical French royalists, agents of the Austrian government, under suspicion of having attempted to assassinate the Queen during the march of the women on Versailles. Taken to Austria, she had been imprisoned and questioned over many months, and finally released for lack of evidence. Back in Paris – where a general amnesty had put an end to enquiries into the events of October 5 and 6 – she was flinging herself again into politics with an energy made more hectic by her recent sufferings.

The vaulted hall of the Jacobin Club was packed to hear her tell her story which had revived and increased her reputation as a heroine of the Left. "The society," reported Brissot's paper *Le Patriote Français*, "expressed the liveliest indignation against her infamous persecutors [the Austrian government] and the utmost admiration for her fortitude. This lover of liberty had pointed out the only way we can ensure our own – to carry the war beyond our frontiers against the despots who threatened us, and who fear it more than us."

In the months of mounting war fever which led up to April 20, Théroigne de Méricourt would be in the forefront of those women who, in one way or another, wished to show their solidarity with the Revolution and their desire to participate in its defence. Paris had changed since she left it in 1790. Her own club, Les Amis de la Loi, had failed through lack of membership and funds. "I had neither the talent nor the experience," she noted ruefully, "and above all I was a woman." But from the summer of 1790, in parallel to the political clubs of the day, a number of "fraternal" or mixed clubs were founded in which women were accepted on equal terms with men. The first of these, the Société Fraternelle des Patriotes des Deux Sexes, was housed in the crypt of the Jacobins Club; it was followed by others in almost all the Paris sections. At the same time clubs for women only were formed in numerous provincial towns, while in Paris a Dutch feminist, the self-styled Baroness Palm d'Aelders, attempted, unsuccessfully, to create a national network of women's clubs, with corresponding branches throughout France.

Originally formed to spread the message of the Revolution more widely, with a special emphasis on questions of welfare and political education, these clubs would change their character with the approach of war. From henceforth, like their masculine equivalents, they were dedicated to the country's defence, both from enemies without and within. Women members joined in patriotic rallies, they petitioned (vainly) for the right to take up arms, they met together to make clothes and bandages for the army. The word *tricoteuse*, of infamous association, originally applied to all those women who knitted for the troops – some of whom, when the time came, would take their work to the foot of the guillotine.

Théroigne de Méricourt was one of the first to demand that the women of Paris, like the men, should be armed. On March 25, addressing the fraternal club of the Faubourg Saint-Antoine, she proposed that they should form a regiment of "amazons", who would train twice weekly in the Champs Elysées. "Let us arm ourselves," she cried in what was virtually a feminist manifesto, " . . . Let us show men that we are not their inferiors in courage or in virtue. . . . Let us rise to the level of our destinies and break our chains; it is high time that women emerged from the shameful state of nullity and ignorance to which the arrogance and injustice of men have so long condemned them. Let us return to the days when the women of Gaul debated with men in the public assemblies, and fought side by side with their husbands against the enemies of liberty. Our conduct at Versailles on October 5 and 6 and numerous decisive and important occasions since proves that we are not strangers to noble and magnanimous sentiments. . . . Why should we not compete with men? Do they alone deserve the glory? . . . We too wish to gain a civic crown and claim the right to die for liberty, a liberty perhaps still dearer to us since our sufferings under despotism have been greater."

Even among her own sex Théroigne's call to arms met with little support. A few days later, attempting to rally the women of the quarter in the streets, she narrowly escaped a beating from a hostile crowd. The royalist papers, regretting that she had not been hanged in Austria, made mock of her military aspirations. "The martial ardour," wrote *Le Petit Gautier*, "which the she-ass of the Jacobins, the demoiselle Théroigne, brought to commanding the patriotic manoeuvres of the ladies about to shed their blood for the members of the National Assembly, was so great that the moustaches of the said demoiselle fell off, and were nowhere to be found."

Once more the butt of the right wing press Théroigne de Méricourt took her place with Madame de Staël and other "vestals of the nation" in a series of skits and caricatures. She appeared as the Queen of Spades in a pack of "patriotic" playing cards; she was depicted in her boudoir, in a tricolour negligé, awaiting the arrival of her lovers: "On her dressing table a pot of vegetable rouge, a dagger, a few scanty curls, a pair of pistols, the *Almanach du Père Gérard*, a hat, the *Declaration of the Rights of Man*, a red woollen bonnet. . . . At the back of the room, a camp bed and straw mattress which serves as a couch for the fair patriot and her numerous admirers. . . ."

The persistent ridicule to which she was subjected could provoke Théroigne to fury. One day, in the gallery of the Feuillants Club, when a member made a joke at her expense, she leapt over the barrier, rushed on to the rostrum and demanded the right to reply. The meeting broke up in tumult and her response was never heard. More successful was her appearance at the Paris Commune, when together with the playwright Joseph Chénier, and the painter David, she proposed a public celebration to welcome the soldiers of Châteauvieux to Paris. (These soldiers, sent to the galleys for mutiny in the early stages of the Revolution, had now been released as public heroes.) Carlyle depicts her leaning on the arm of Joseph Chénier, a celebrity in full enjoyment of her fame. There is no record of her having been present at the celebrations for the soldiers of Châteauvieux, though women indeed took part in the procession, and a hundred young girls, "dressed as nymphs and just as beautiful", drew the chains of the former prisoners through the streets.

It was in such decorative roles that most men preferred to see the women of the day. Even the fraternal clubs were regarded by many as a threat. The men of the Faubourg Saint-Antoine, for instance, denounced Théroigne for encouraging women to attend them. "They would far rather," said one orator, "come home to find their house in order than await their wives' return from meetings, where they do not always gain in sweetness or good temper." "We don't teach you how to love your children," complained the anti-feminist *Révolutions de Paris*; "kindly refrain from coming to our clubs to teach us the duties of a citizen."

★ ★ ★

While Théroigne expended her energies in public, constantly frustrated, as she put it, by the "strength of masculine arrogance and prejudice", Madame Roland behind the scenes serenely held the reins of power. Long accustomed to share her husband's work, she continued to do so during his ministry. Looking back from her prison cell a year later, she assessed her contribution without false modesty.

"I did not involve myself in the work of administration," she wrote, "but if it was a question of a circular, an instruction or an important public announcement, we conferred together in our usual way and then, imbued with his ideas and nourished by my own, I took up the pen which I had more time than he to wield. . . . Without me, Roland would have been a no less able administrator; his activity, his knowledge, his honesty were his own; with me he made a greater impression because I brought to his writing that mixture of strength and sweetness, of reasoned authority and the charm of sentiment of which, perhaps, only a woman, gifted with sensibility and good taste, is capable."

The Rolands were now installed in their official residence, a magnificent establishment in the rue Neuve des Petits Champs, formerly the Contrôle Général or Treasury. Here Madame Necker had once held sway and here Madame Roland, in a very different way, would establish her reign as a political hostess, gathering round her once more the circle of admiring Girondins whose inspiration she had been in earlier days. The salon of the "Dame Coco", as the scurrilous *Père Duchesne* described her, was a centre of Girondin debate.

Ostensibly at least Madame Roland refused to be impressed by the grandeur of her surroundings, the sweeping marble staircases, the vast salon with its chandeliers and mirrors, the bedroom where the matrimonial bed was crowned with ostrich feathers and painted gods and goddesses disported themselves on the walls and ceiling. She chose the smallest of the string of reception rooms as her headquarters, installing herself discreetly with her books and desk and since, as she put it, she and Roland shared a perfect community of opinions and information, many visitors who sought the minister's ear found it easiest to come direct to her. Twice a week she gave a dinner for colleagues, deputies and other ministers, maintaining her policy of listening but not joining in the political discussions round her. "Taste and neatness without profusion adorned my table," she wrote, "and ostentatious luxury was unknown." As a matter of principle she did not ask other women; she had no desire to run a salon like that of Dumouriez' mistress, Madame de Beauvert, where the company was mixed and the atmosphere far removed from the puritan simplicity she favoured.

Dumouriez she frankly distrusted. He had the graceful manners and easy morals of a courtier of the old regime. Witty, cynical and worldly, he seemed the antithesis of Madame Roland's austere and upright husband, whose brusque uncompromising manner fell little short of rudeness and who even in his appearance made no concessions to convention. When he arrived for his first interview with the King he wore his usual Quaker-like garb of shabby black, with a round hat, woollen stockings and sturdy laced up shoes. The master of ceremonies looked at him aghast. "Monsieur has no buckles on his shoes," he whispered to Dumouriez. "In that case," said Dumouriez coolly, "all is lost."

Between Dumouriez and the sternly righteous Madame Roland it was unlikely that there would ever be much sympathy. Far more akin to her in temperament, or so it still seemed to her then, was Robespierre, the "Incorruptible", once an ally, now openly in opposition to the Girondin ministry from which he and his supporters had been excluded. It was their attitude towards the war which had first divided them. For Robespierre, war was a rash and dangerous step, which he had consistently opposed in the debates leading up to its outbreak. In sombre language he pointed out its dangers, the country's unpreparedness, the suspect loyalty of aristocratic officers, the ambivalent attitude of the King. He saw, which was true, that in leading the agitation for war the Girondins were seeking to establish their own political ascendancy. At the same time, by taking office under the King, they laid themselves open to accusations of treachery and complicity with the court.

Madame Roland saw Robespierre's opposition to the war in personal rather than ideological terms. "Robespierre, ardent, jealous, avid for popularity, envious of the success of others," she wrote later, " . . . set out to make himself the chief of the party which opposed the declaration of war." Her first hope was to bring him round, or at least soften his views. Within the first few days of Roland's ministry she invited him to call on her, assuring him of her continuing admiration and esteem. The interview does not seem to have gone well. Robespierre, stiff and cold, remained impervious to his hostess's eloquence and charm. In the Jacobin club and in the press he continued his violent attacks on the Girondins.

In many ways, despite the rift now opening between their parties, Madame Roland's views came closer to Robespierre's. Like him she had no faith in the idea of a constitutional monarchy or the good intentions of the King. It seemed to her impossible that the King, brought up in the despotic traditions of his ancestors, should willingly accept a constitution which virtually stripped him of his powers. When Roland, after his first audience with the King, returned full of praise for his co-operativeness and courtesy, his wife rebuked him for his gullibility. The King was wasting his minister's time, she told him, deliberately holding up decisions by a display of affability and vagueness, and she brushed aside those who tried to defend him by reminding them of the flight to Varennes.

Events soon forced the King to take up a position. The war had begun disastrously. The French army, ill-prepared and under strength, was in retreat and disarray. In Paris the economic situation was deteriorating, food riots seemed to presage severer outbreaks of mob violence. Partly to control the situation, partly to intimidate the King, whom they cast with court and clergy as scapegoats for their setbacks, the Girondin ministry proposed the setting up of a camp of twenty thousand *fédérés*, or provincial volunteers, outside the capital. A second decree, intended to prevent subversion, proposed the deportation without trial of refractory or non-juring priests. To the King, the threatening presence of twenty thousand volunteers, whose loyalty was highly suspect, was wholly unacceptable; so too, as a matter of conscience, was the decree against the priests. Intending to refuse his sanction to both decrees, and hoping that French defeats would weaken the position of the Girondins, he played for time as long as possible.

For Madame Roland the King's delay was final evidence of his bad faith. Having failed to rally her husband's fellow ministers in a joint protest she prevailed on him to remonstrate alone. It was she however who took up the pen. In a letter mingling menaces with exhortation, dashed off, as she wrote later, "in a single sitting", she rebuked the King for his intransigence. The Revolution, she wrote, had begun in men's minds, it would be carried through in blood if wiser counsels did not prevail. If the King, in refusing to pass the decrees, left his loyalty to the Constitution in doubt, the nation, already in a state of ferment, would take the law into its own hands. "I know," she concluded, "that the austere language of truth is seldom heard close to the throne. I also know that it is because it is not heard that revolutions become necessary."

This letter, "sublime" in the eyes of some historians, high-handed and insolent in those of others, was signed by Roland and presented to the King on June 10. Three days later, in a curt two line note, the King dismissed his minister, and on June 19 informed the National Assembly of his veto against the two decrees. The Rolands meanwhile had lost no time in publicising their protest. The letter was read out in the National Assembly where, amidst applause, it was voted that it should be printed and circulated throughout France. The obscure and pedantic Roland had become a hero overnight. "I had not been proud at his entry into the ministry," wrote Madame Roland; "I was so at his exit."

Roland's dismissal had been followed almost immediately by that of his fellow Girondins. Madame Roland had been their inspiration, passionate in her devotion to the cause of liberty, but woefully deficient in practical experience of politics or the great forces unleashed by the war. It was a criticism that could be launched at all the Girondins, idealistic, intellectual, but inadequate to their destiny. They had pushed their country into war, they had now pushed the monarchy to the brink. It would not survive their fall for long. On June 20, the anniversary of the Tennis Court oath, the crowd, inflamed by the news of the King's double veto, broke into the Tuileries, invading the royal apartments, forcing the King to wear a cap of liberty and to drink the nation's health. Though Madame Roland might reflect with satisfaction on the spectacular aftermath of the Girondins' downfall, and the part she had played in it, she was soon to realise that by calling up mob violence the Girondins had handed the initiative to extremists more ruthless than themselves.

For the time being the Rolands retired into private life, leaving behind them the splendours of a ministry whose physical attributes at least had done little to seduce them. Madame Roland left its gilded salons, its tapestries and mirrors, with scarcely a backward glance. "I never thought of them," she wrote, "as anything more than the furnishings of an inn." But in the weeks of rising tension which followed the invasion of the Tuileries her eyes were fixed firmly on the prospect of their return to power.

Chapter 7

"You will soon hear the details of the insult offered to the King," wrote Narbonne to his chief of staff, Alexandre d'Arblay, three days after the invasion of the Tuileries. "It is no longer possible for a man of honour to remain inactive if the whole of France does not denounce this outrage."

Since his dismissal as Minister of War, Narbonne had joined the army on the northern frontier under the command of Lafayette. Madame de Staël, so rumour had it, had gone to join him at the camp of Arras, bearing a phial of poison on her person, with the intention of killing herself should any harm come to her lover. How Narbonne responded to this gesture is not known; his overwhelming preoccupation now was with the King. His liberalism was sincere, but so too was the loyalty he felt as a soldier and a nobleman to the monarchy, a loyalty which transcended the King's personal defects, and in which his own honour was closely involved.

Madame de Staël shared his anxiety. "Greatly agitated by the horrible scenes which had taken place, and by those which were in preparation," she put forward a plan with Narbonne for the royal family's escape. It involved the purchase of an estate near Dieppe, and two preliminary journeys there, each time with a man, woman and child, answering roughly to the description of the King, Queen and Dauphin, who on the third journey would take their place, and then take ship to England. The plan, like a similar one proposed by Lafayette, who hoped to transfer the royal family to safety in the midst of the army at Compiègne, was rejected. To the King and Marie Antoinette such liberal nobles as Lafayette and Narbonne were as much anathema as the wildest Jacobins. Already resigned to their probable fate, they placed their last remaining hope in rescue by the invading armies of Austria and Prussia.

The brief upsurge of sympathy which had swept the country at the King's ordeal at the hands of the mob was quickly dissipated. Suspicion (well founded) that the King was intriguing with the enemy, the fear of invasion, and on July 11 the declaration of a state of national emergency, all played into the hands of those who sought to overthrow the monarchy. In the National Assembly, in the clubs and press the court and royal family were daily reviled for their treachery. "On all sides," wrote Madame de Staël, "one heard insults directed against the palace of kings; nothing protected it any more but a sort of respect which still served as a barrier against this ancient dwelling; but at any moment this barrier might be broken and then all would be lost."

The arrival in Paris of the *fédérés* from the provinces for the Fête de la Fédération on July 14 brought further menace to the situation. Their presence in a permanent camp outside the city had been vetoed by the King; it was unlikely that his veto could continue to carry weight for long. Madame de Staël was present at the celebrations in the Champ de Mars as the columns of *fédérés*, ragged and threatening, marched past the platform on which the King and royal family were standing. The Queen's eyes, she wrote, were blinded by tears; the expression on her face was something she would never forget. Amidst the shouts of the crowd for Pétion, the Jacobin mayor of Paris, the few faint voices that cried "*Vive le roi!*" had the sound of a last adieu.

The days of the monarchy were now numbered. Too late the Girondins, who had sought a peaceful transition to a republic, realised that events were out of their control. The manifesto of the Duke of Brunswick, now commanding the allied forces, threatening Paris with destruction if the royal family were harmed, sparked the fuse of an already explosive situation. Narbonne, accused of treason in the Jacobin Club, had returned to Paris in secret. Together with other liberal noblemen, those friends who in happier days had flocked to Madame de Staël's salon, he prepared to defend the Tuileries to the last. All offers of help having been refused by the court, they would form an unofficial patrol outside the palace when the time came, "exposing themselves to massacre", as Madame de Staël expressed it, "in order to console themselves for not being able to fight".

On the night of August 9–10 the storm broke. Shortly before midnight the bells of the forty-eight sections of Paris began to sound, calling the town to arms. That evening the Paris Commune had been disbanded; an insurrectionary Commune had taken its place; the order had gone out to march on the Tuileries. All through the night, a night of stifling heat, the monotonous sound of the tocsin continued. Madame de Staël, sleepless at the window of the Swedish embassy, waited hourly for news of her lover and his friends. At seven in the morning the first rumblings of cannon from the section were heard; the attack on the Tuileries had begun.

★   ★   ★

The events of August 10, the storming of the Tuileries, the massacre of the Swiss guard, the sack of the palace, took their blood-stained course. Through the fury of the day the figure of Théroigne de Méricourt, in her habitual riding habit, pistols and sabre by her side, could be seen in the forefront of the mob. It is thus that Baudelaire, his imagination captured by her legend, evoked her half a century later:

> . . . *Théroigne, amante de carnage*
> *Excitant à l'assaut un peuple sans souliers*. . . .

For her part in August 10 Théroigne would be awarded a civic crown. It is not possible to follow her course in detail through the day though we know that she was present when, the Swiss guard having been ordered to cease firing by the King, the gates of the palace were stormed and the mob surged in. But she is recalled most vividly in various accounts when, earlier in the day, the royalist journalist Suleau was arrested on the terrace of the Feuillants, under suspicion of being part of a royalist patrol. A number of suspects had already been rounded up, and a crowd outside the Feuillants monastery where they were imprisoned was calling for their deliverance to the "justice of the people". An official who vainly tried to reason with them was shouted down. At that moment Théroigne arrived, dressed in red, with a hat with tricolour plumes, and mounting the trestle he had just left, urged the crowd to massacre the prisoners. "I saw, with a sort of horror," wrote a witness to the scene, "that she was pretty, very pretty, her excitement enhanced her beauty . . . she was in the throes of a revolutionary hysteria impossible to describe."

It is a description that may have gained in the telling. Caught up in the collective madness of the day, and rendered unstable by her sufferings in Austria, Théroigne was perhaps already showing signs of the insanity to which she would later succumb. What seems certain is that the crowd, exhorted by Théroigne, grew so insistent that despite the fact that he had two hundred soldiers at his command, the section commander released the prisoners to their mercy. They were hacked down as they came out one by one. Suleau, the fourth to emerge, was the particular object of Théroigne's fury. The most celebrated journalist of the Right, his bitter, biting pen had long been the scourge of the Girondins and Jacobins alike. It was in his paper, *Les Actes des Apôtres*, that Théroigne had been most often pilloried. On seeing him, say some accounts, Théroigne leapt at his throat. Shaking her off, Suleau seized a sabre, and defended himself heroically against the crowd till he in turn was cut down. His body, together with that of eight other prisoners, was decapitated, and their heads mounted on pikes.

★　★　★

Throughout the morning of August 10 Madame de Staël, with a little group of friends, waited breathlessly for news of Narbonne and his companions. Towards afternoon reports came through that they had all been massacred in the storming of the Tuileries. Setting out immediately in her coach to find out more, she made her way to the Pont Royal but was stopped by a handful of men on the bridge who made it clear from their expressive gestures that scenes of slaughter were taking place on the other side. After two hours of useless efforts to cross over, she at last got word that all those in whom she was most interested were still alive, but that most had gone into hiding to escape arrest.

That evening she set out on foot to the various obscure houses where they had taken refuge, passing doorways in which armed men and women, worn out by the day's carnage, lay sprawled in drunken stupor. The appearance of a patrol designed to keep order was a signal for all honest men to flee. Keeping order in this context, she wrote, meant clearing the path for further killing.

Devoted and loyal as she was to all her friends, Madame de Staël's chief concern, as she made her way through the dark streets, was for Narbonne. As a leading constitutionalist his arrest and imprisonment were certain should he be discovered. He had found a temporary hiding place, but dared not endanger his hosts by remaining there. The Swedish embassy, though its immunity was far from certain, offered his best hope of safety. He arrived there late the following evening. "He was pale as death though still elegantly dressed," recalled the embassy chaplain Pastor Gambs, who remembered him from earlier meetings as a "stiff and haughty cavalier". Now, fearing imminent pursuit, he spent the night beneath the altar in the embassy chapel, emerging the next morning, noted Gambs, in a considerably less brilliant state than before.

Gambs had not been altogether displeased to see the former Minister of War at a disadvantage, but it was thanks to his help that Madame de Staël was able to arrange for his escape. Having made discreet enquiries in the German speaking community he produced a young Hanoverian doctor, Justus Erich Bollman, who pronounced himself ready to undertake the enterprise. Bollman, adventurous and quixotic, was deeply impressed by Narbonne, and by the energy and courage of Madame de Staël on his behalf. The fact that she was six months pregnant – she was expecting a baby by Narbonne – only added to his admiration, which remained however purely platonic.

"A crowd of motives among which the beauty of Madame de

Staël was not one – for she was ugly – rushed through my mind," he wrote later. "The joy of saving such a man, so handsome, so noble and so calm, the satisfaction of restoring this woman's peace of mind . . . the prospect of reaching England and bettering my position, the charm of the unusual – all these, against which I could only balance the danger to my life, acted on me simultaneously, transforming a possibility into a firm resolve."

It was not a moment too soon to think of Narbonne's escape. On the very day that notices denouncing him were posted in the rue du Bac the street was closed by soldiers and a search party demanded entrance to the embassy. Narbonne and another fugitive were hidden in an upstairs room. Madame de Staël confronted the searchers with terror in her heart.

"I began by frightening them as much as possible," she wrote, "with the idea that they were committing a breach of international law in entering the house of an ambassador. As they knew very little geography I persuaded them that Sweden, being a major power on France's frontier, would launch an immediate attack if provoked."

Seeing that her arguments were making an impression, she switched her tone, and began to joke with them on the injustice of their suspicions. "Nothing pleases people of that class more than joking, for even at the height of their fury against the aristocracy they are always pleased to be treated as an equal by them. In this way I was able to lead them back to the door, and I thanked God for the extraordinary strength he had given me at that moment."

The respite could only be a brief one. Narbonne's liaison with Madame de Staël was common knowledge; sooner or later determined searchers would return. Meanwhile the issue of passports had been suspended, the exits from the town were guarded and the number of arrests was rising daily. The resourceful Bollman, however, had managed to obtain the passport of a Hanoverian friend which, issued by the British embassy – Hanover being still attached to the British crown – enabled Narbonne to travel as an Englishman. Disguised and in company with Bollman, he managed to pass the various guardposts on the journey to

Boulogne, feigning indolence or sleepiness while Bollman engaged the guards in conversation. They crossed the Channel in three hours – "Narbonne rendered up all he had eaten," noted Bollman – and arrived in Dover on August 20. From there, the next day, they made their way to London.

"You have saved my life and more than my life," wrote Madame de Staël to Bollman when she heard the news of their arrival, while to Narbonne in a letter radiant with relief, she described the dangers he had just escaped: "Those cruel men [the commissaries of the insurrectionary Commune] had sworn to kill you, they pretended to have found papers which compromised you horribly, and totally unjust as it was, felt sure of being able to condemn you."

In view of her pregnancy and the scandal it would cause if she arrived in England without her husband she would not be able to join Narbonne in England till after her baby was born. She planned to complete her pregnancy in Switzerland and where her parents were anxiously awaiting her. Necker, wrote their friend and neighbour Edward Gibbon, was "in a state of agitation and affliction impossible to imagine". His fears had been made worse by a recent letter from Madame de Staël; the situation in Paris must be truly alarming, he told Gibbon, for his daughter, who never knew fear or checked her words, had written in tones of the utmost tact and moderation.

Madame de Staël awaited the passports that would make her departure possible in an atmosphere of mounting terror and alarm. Enemy forces had crossed the frontiers; the prisons were overflowing with suspects; already there were rumours of a projected massacre. Her fears for Narbonne assuaged, her chief concern was for her other friends. Several had taken refuge in the embassy; Talleyrand, recently returned from his diplomatic mission in England, was desperately seeking an official passport to return there. He would receive one, on the thinnest of excuses, on September 7. Other friends, less fortunate, were already in prison: the Comte de Jaucourt and the Marquis de Lally Tollendal, both former constitutionalists, had been arrested after August 10. It was on their behalf that, regardless of her pregnancy and her own precarious position, Madame de Staël would expend herself most fervently. Running through the list of members of the new Commune, whom she knew only by reputation, her choice fell on the public prosecutor, Pierre Louis Manuel, who, having literary pretensions, might perhaps be helpful to a *femme de lettres*. If it was not true, as one account later had it, that Madame de Staël produced a dagger from her bodice and threatened to stab herself if her friends were not released, her pleas in any case were eloquent enough to be successful. Lally Tollendal was released on August 31, Jaucourt the following day. Twenty four hours later, while the tocsin sounded once more from all over Paris, the massacres in the prisons would begin.

Chapter 8

The fall of the monarchy of August 10, though orchestrated by the extremists of the Left, had had as its first result the return of the Girondins to power. Together with the two fellow ministers dismissed by Louis XVI Roland resumed his place in the ministry, but a newcomer, one of the foremost actors in the attack on the Tuileries, was appointed Minister of Justice. It was Danton, now come to the fore from a past which Madame Roland would scornfully describe in her memoirs.

"If I had kept to a simple narrative," she wrote, "instead of letting my pen roam at large over events, I would have taken Danton at the beginning of 1789, a miserable lawyer, richer in debts than briefs . . . I would have shown him rising in his section, which was then called a district, by the strength of his lungs; a great supporter of the Orléans party, enjoying a growing affluence that year, without any sign of the work that ought to have produced it . . . I would have pointed him out declaiming in the popular clubs, declaring himself the defender of the rights of all . . . appearing on August 10 with those returning from the Tuileries, and arriving at the Ministry as a tribune favoured by the people, whose appointment to the government was necessary to satisfy them."

A mutual antipathy from the first sprung up between them. Rigidly honest, both she and her husband were horrified by Danton's extravagance and the corruption he scarcely bothered to conceal. Physical repulsion, too, played a part. Danton, pock-marked, hideous, his mouth distorted by a scar from a childhood accident, exuded a vitality so powerful it was almost a tangible force. No one, wrote Madame Roland, could display a greater zeal for liberty. But on looking at his face she found it impossible, however hard she tried, to believe it that of an honest man. "I have never seen anything which so perfectly expressed the violence of brutal passions and an astonishing audacity, half veiled by an air of great joviality and the affectation of frankness and good fellowship."

At the beginning they did their best to get on, and Danton called almost every day at the Ministry of the Interior, often pausing for a bowl of soup with Madame Roland. Never had there been a greater need for unity. The King, suspended since August 10, was a prisoner in the Temple. The insurrectionary Commune and the clubs of Paris made inroads on the tottering authority of the National Assembly. The armies of Austria and Prussia were streaming across the frontiers. Obsessed by the idea of Danton's dishonesty – she suspected him, rightly, of lining his pockets with government money – Madame Roland failed to recognise the qualities that would make him, quite literally, France's saviour in its hour of danger. While Danton sought to rally the nation, exhorting his countrymen in the National Assembly to "dare and dare and dare again," the Rolands' chief concern was the distribution of funds for propaganda along Girondist lines. When the violently left wing Marat asked the Rolands for a contribution towards the expenses of his paper his request was peremptorily refused. He found his funds elsewhere from the Duc d'Orléans, now known as Philippe Egalité, and used his paper to take revenge. His *Lettre sur Madame Roland*, ridiculing her husband as a cuckold, appeared on September 2. It was a day that was to have a far more sinister significance. That afternoon, at about five o'clock, the massacre in the prisons began.

Danton's responsibility for the September massacres, the massacres which in his own words put "a river of blood" between Paris and the army of the emigrés, has been much disputed. As far as Madame Roland was concerned, there was no doubt of his guilt, and reporting the words of the prison inspector, Jean Grandpré, she tells in her memoirs how Grandpré, appalled by the butchery that was taking place, sought out Danton as he emerged from the day's council. Cutting short his urgent protests, and with a gesture to accompany his words, Danton cried out, "I don't give a f . . . for the prisoners. Let them fend for themselves."

For five days the killing in the prisons went on. Under the pretext that the prisoners were counter-revolutionaries, preparing to fall on the population of Paris as the enemy armies advanced, more than 1,200 prisoners, some merely children, were murdered by a mob of a few hundred. The authorities, perhaps because they were unable to, did nothing to prevent the massacres. On September 3 Roland, in a vain protest, called for the re-establishment of order. But his own position was precarious in the extreme. The night before an angry crowd had surrounded the Ministry of the Interior demanding arms. A warrant for his arrest had been issued by the Vigilance Committee, then later rescinded by Danton who, perhaps, sought reconciliation with the Girondins. Madame Roland classed him already with the extremists of the Left. "We are under the blade of Robespierre and Marat," she wrote to a friend on October 5; "these people are doing everything to incite the people and to turn them against the National Assembly and the Council. . . . They maintain a small army, paid for by what they have stolen from the Tuileries, or what they are given by Danton, who behind the scenes is the leader of the gang." Looking back on the horrors of those five days the worst horror, it seemed to her, was that nothing was done to stop them. "All Paris looked on," she wrote, "and all Paris is accursed in my eyes. I no longer hope that liberty can be established among cowards . . . cold spectators of murders which the courage of fifty men could easily have prevented."

★ ★ ★

On the morning of September 2, having at last received passports for herself and her servants, Madame de Staël had made her preparations to leave Paris. She had one last service to render as she did so. The Abbé de Montesquiou, a cousin of Narbonne, was in hourly danger of arrest; she had arranged that he would travel with her using the papers of a servant. A few days earlier the frontier town of Longwy had fallen to the enemy and that morning news had come of the probable fall of Verdun. While the bells of the Paris sections rang out the alarm that would be the signal for the massacres, Madame de Staël, in her ambassadorial coach, with six men in livery, set out from the embassy. She had deliberately planned to travel in as grand a style as possible, hoping that by underlining her diplomatic status her passage would be made easier. She could hardly have been more mistaken. Scarcely had she left the embassy than a swarm of "hags from hell" fell on the coach, dragging the horses to a stop, and crying that she was carrying off the nation's gold. A crowd quickly gathered, and the order was given that she should be taken before the assembly of her local section, the Faubourg Saint-Germain. With just time to whisper to a servant to warn the Abbé of what had happened, she was taken before the assembly and ordered to present herself at the Hôtel de Ville.

The journey to the Hôtel de Ville took over two hours. Her coach was surrounded all along the route by crowds of people yelling for her death – not that they knew her personally, she wrote, but that the sight of a coach and liveries were enough to arouse their fury. The fact that she was heavily pregnant gained her no sympathy, if anything it inflamed them further. Outside the Hôtel de Ville, where the steps were crowded with armed men, a pike was levelled at her, and had it not been parried by a gendarme, would undoubtedly have killed her.

Inside the Hôtel de Ville Robespierre, with two secretaries, was presiding over the session on a platform raised above the throng who filled the chamber and whose cries of "*Vive la nation!*" came near to drowning the proceedings. Madame de Staël, half fainting, was given a place beside a slight acquaintance, the bailiff of Virieu; he rose to his feet on seeing her, declaring that he did not know her and that her affairs had nothing to do with him. "The poor man's lack of chivalry displeased me," she admitted, "and I became all the more anxious to defend myself seeing that he had no desire to save me the trouble. I got up therefore and made plain the right I had to leave Paris as the ambassadress of Sweden, showing the passports which had been given to me in recognition of this right."

At this point the prosecutor, Manuel, arrived. Horrified at seeing her in such circumstances, he made himself responsible for her, conducting her and her maid to a little room behind the hall. They stayed there for six hours, she wrote, dying of hunger, thirst and fear. Through the window in the square below they could see the mob returning from the prisons, their bare and bloodstained arms showing only too clearly what work they had been up to. Meanwhile, in the chamber, the suspicion that she might have been helping Narbonne to escape made the question of her diplomatic immunity far from certain but finally, for fear of providing an incident with Sweden, it was decided to let her go. Late at night – he had not dared to come earlier for fear of the crowd – Manuel came to conduct her home in his coach. The street lamps were not lit, but there were groups of men carrying torches through the street whose light, she wrote, was far more frightening than the darkness. From time to time their coach was stopped but Manuel's firm announcement that he was the representative of the Commune brought them safely home.

The next day, with passports for herself and one servant only, she was able to leave Paris. Tallien, secretary of the Commune, came to escort her to the city gates. On entering her rooms in the embassy he could not fail to recognise a number of suspected persons, whose presence she begged him not to reveal. He kept his word, she noted.

She set off on the road to Switzerland. Behind her the prison massacres were entering their second day. Outside the window of the Queen in the Temple the bleeding head of the Princesse de Lamballe was paraded on a pike.

"As I drew further from the capital," wrote Madame de Staël, "the violence of the tempest seemed to abate, and in the mountains of the Jura nothing recalled the dreadful scenes of which Paris was the theatre. On every side, however, I heard the

French exhorted to repel the foreign foe. I confess that in that moment I could see no enemy save the murderers to whose mercy I had left my friends, the royal family and all the decent folk of France."

Chapter 9

The September massacres which in Danton's words had put a river of blood between Paris and the army of the émigrés, had set a great gulf too between the high ideals of those who, like Madame Roland, had identified themselves with the Revolution and the realities they now confronted. "If you knew the terrible details!" wrote Madame Roland to a friend. "Women brutally violated before being torn to pieces by those tigers, entrails cut out and carried like ribbons, people eating human flesh. . . . You know my enthusiasm for the Revolution, well now I am ashamed of it. It has been dishonoured by scoundrels, it has become hideous to me." Roland, whose vain attempts to control events had merely underlined his ineffectiveness, had lacked the courage to condemn them outright. "Yesterday," he wrote, on September 3, "was a day over which it is perhaps best to draw a veil. I know that the people, terrible in their vengeance, were carrying out a sort of justice." But the shock of what had happened made him ill, his skin grew yellow, he scarcely ate or slept, he buried himself in work. Increasingly alarmed at the Assembly's impotence in the face of the Paris Commune and the mob, he contemplated the government's removal to a safer place. The accusation that the Girondins planned to abandon Paris in flight from the enemy would later be one of the main charges against them.

In the aftermath of the massacres a deathly chill fell over Paris' social life. The liberal aristocracy had fled if they were not in prison or in hiding; the leading embassies were closed; the gregarious Gouverneur Morris, who even after the sack of the Tuileries had continued to be entertained in the salons of a few remaining hostesses, had no more social gatherings to report. Those aristocrats who remained behind, Mesdames de Fontenay and de Beauharnais among them, lay low or sought friends among the men of the new order. The morals of both had always been easy – Madame de Fontenay in particular was notorious for the number of her lovers – and the fate of so many round them put the art of survival at a premium.

Joséphine de Beauharnais, not long returned to France from the West Indies, had never taken a great interest in politics. "You know," she once remarked, "I am too indolent to take sides." But her husband, Alexandre de Beauharnais, who had been the president of the National Assembly at the time of the flight to Varennes, was now chief of staff in the army of the Rhine. Though she was officially separated from him, the relationship still worked to her advantage, bringing her into contact with the rising figures of the Left. Among them was Jean-Lambert Tallien, the new secretary of the Commune – the same who had escorted Madame de Staël from Paris. He was twenty-six, good looking unscrupulous, deeply implicated in the September massacres, but soon to become an important figure in her life and still more in that of Madame de Fontenay.

Thérésia de Fontenay's position was less secure than Joséphine's. She had been a celebrity in the earlier days of the Revolution, moving leftward with the tide of the times, a familiar presence in the galleries of the National Assembly. She could still be seen occasionally in the audience of the National Convention, which replaced the old Assembly, and would glimpse there, perhaps for the first time, the perorating figure of Tallien. But she no longer wished to draw attention to herself. Her husband's title had been abolished, but lacking the revolutionary credentials of Alexandre de Beauharnais it remained a dangerous liability. Through the autumn of 1792 he and his wife sought to stay in favour with the aid of a series of voluntary "loans" to the nation – Thérésia divesting herself even down to the contents of her wardrobe. But by the beginning of the following year the situation had grown so menacing that they were forced to leave Paris, the Marquis to escape into exile, his wife to join her Spanish family in the comparative safety – as she thought – of Bordeaux. It was there, one year later, as the Terror reached its height, that her path would first cross Tallien's.

*   *   *

On September 2, 1792, the new National Convention, elected to take the place of the Legislative Assembly, forgathered for the first time. Roland, representing the Somme, was among the deputies for the provinces where the Girondins were in the majority. Paris was solidly in the hands of the Left, with Robespierre, Marat and Danton among its representatives. (For a time Danton, like Roland, continued to hold his ministerial post as well.) Meanwhile the tide of war was turning. On September 20 the revolutionary army, under Dumouriez, turned back the Prussian advance at Valmy – a victory which, in the words of Goethe, marked the beginning of a new era in the history of the world. By October 8 the last foreign troops had been driven back across the frontiers. For the time being the Girondins, their war policy vindicated, regained their political ascendancy. Madame Roland, her attitude to Dumouriez transformed by the brilliance of his generalship, greeted him with unfamiliar warmth when he returned to Paris, while Dumouriez, responding in kind, arrived at the Ministry of the Interior with a bunch of flowers for his hostess.

Strengthened by the army's successes the Girondins found courage at last to express their horror at the September massacres and to turn their guns against Robespierre and the extremists of the Left – the Mountain, as they were known from their position on the highest benches of the chamber. A stream of Girondin propaganda poured from the Ministry of the Interior. In the National Convention the journalist Jean-Baptiste Louvet, urged on by Madame Roland, stood up to accuse Robespierre of complicity in the massacres and of seeking to become a dictator. (His speech denouncing him was printed by Roland at government expense.) Robespierre, recoiling under Louvet's attack, had demanded a week's grace to reply. His coolly reasoned answer, when it came, cut through the eloquent but vaguely worded charges of his accuser and perversely served to strengthen his position in the Convention.

The fight, however, was going out of Roland. Personal troubles were overshadowing his political concerns. The wife who for twelve years had made his welfare her chief duty, subsuming herself in his work, and keeping all admirers at a discreet platonic distance, had fallen overwhelmingly in love. It was not in her character to give way to her passion. At a time when the fever and dangers of the Revolution had everywhere called conventional morality into question, she preserved the same firm sense of right and wrong which had always been the basis of her conduct. But it was not in her character either to keep the truth from her husband, and her confession when she made it dealt him a devastating blow.

"I honour, I cherish my husband, as a good daughter adores a virtuous father, to whom she would sacrifice even a lover," she wrote later in her memoirs. "But I found the man who might have been that lover, and while remaining faithful to my duties I was too frank to hide the sentiments which I subordinated to them. My husband, excessively sensitive, both from affection and *amour propre*, proved unable to bear the idea of the slightest change in my feelings towards him; his imagination darkened, his jealousy irritated me, happiness deserted us; he adored me, I sacrificed myself to him and we were miserable."

At the back of the locket in which she kept his portrait Madame Roland slipped a description of her lover. The words on the faded scrap of paper (now in the municipal library in Versailles) are still legible. They read in part:

"Nature endowed him with a loving soul, a proud spirit and a lofty character. His sensitive nature made him seek peace and the calm of a life of obscurity and domestic virtue. Sorrows of the heart increased the melancholy towards which he was naturally inclined. Circumstances having thrown him into politics, he brought to them the ardour of a fiery courage and the inflexibility of an austere probity."

François Nicolas Buzot, the subject of this eulogy, was thirty-two, six years younger than Madame Roland. Born in Evreux, where he had later practised as a lawyer, he had come to Paris for the States General and had sat as a deputy in the Constituent Assembly. He had first met the Rolands in 1791 when, with Brissot and other future Girondins, he had formed part of the left wing circle that gathered in their apartment. Since then he had served as a judge in the provinces, remaining in touch by correspondence. He had returned to Paris as a deputy in September 1792, and was now a leading member of the Girondins. Unhappily married to an older wife, it had taken little to make him fall in love with Madame Roland, whose ideals and enthusiasms closely matched his own. Rigid and self-righteous, he does not appear as an appealing character to those who read his memoirs. But his republican virtues were precisely those that would appeal to Madame Roland, while his melancholy good looks and obvious devotion aroused in her a passion against which, she wrote, she struggled with the vigour of an athlete.

From the end of October 1792 the Girondins had ceased frequenting the Jacobin Club. The rift between the two parties was now clearly defined. Between them lay the Plain, the mass of uncommitted deputies who occupied the central benches of the National Convention. The approaches of Danton, who could have joined forces with the Girondins to swing opinion against the Jacobins, had been refused. It was Madame Roland's influence, at least in part, that had blocked the alliance. To her instinctive distrust of Danton, to her horror at his attitude to the September massacres, was added a purely personal resentment. In the course of a debate in the National Assembly Danton had remarked sarcastically that Roland was not alone in his ministry, grumbling audibly on returning to his seat that the nation needed ministers who were not led by their wives. Roland himself, obsessed by the idea of Danton's dishonesty, consistently demanded that the minister should account for the large sums of public money that had passed through his hands, and was as consistently rebuffed.

Nowhere were the differences between Girondins and Jacobins more openly revealed than in their attitude towards the King who, imprisoned in the Temple, had remained in virtual limbo from August to November. The Girondins as a party were anxious to spare his life, preferring the alternatives of imprisonment or exile. The Jacobins were determined on his execution. The delays and indecisions which had postponed the question of his trial were dramatically brought to an end on November 20, with the discovery of a secret cache, the famous "iron safe", in a wall of the royal apartments in the Tuileries. Roland, as Minister of the Interior, together with the King's former locksmith and the architect in charge of the palace, had hastened to open the safe and inspect its contents. Amongst the documents it contained were letters proving the King's complicity with the Austrians and compromising several former deputies. It was enough to precipitate his trial; on December 11 the King was summoned to appear before the National Convention.

Meanwhile Roland's ill-judged action in opening the safe without official witnesses gave his opponents the chance to accuse him of abstracting letters incriminating himself and his fellow Girondins. His indignant denials were eventually accepted but the accusation further served to weaken his position. The Jacobin press pursued the smear relentlessly. Throughout the autumn, in the gutter language that endorsed their democratic sympathies, they had made a target of the Rolands, Madame Roland variously depicted as a Messalina and a whore, her salon as a hotbed of intrigue. "The baying Marat has been unloosed on me," wrote Madame Roland gloomily that Christmas; "he doesn't let go for an instant, pamphlets have multiplied and I doubt if even Antoinette [the Queen] has had worse horrors written about her." As the year ended Hébert, Marat's cruder but no less violent counterpart, wrote in his paper, the *Père Duchesne*:

"Well, now it's over, this famous year which should have seen the last of royalty if Roland and Brissot did not exist. . . . A new revolution is brewing. 1793 will finish off the Rolandins and Brissotins. They asked for it, the b . . . s, and like the eels of Melun they're squealing before they're even hurt."

★ ★ ★

In December 1792, after a fifteen month absence, Madame de la Tour du Pin returned to France. In the period of relative calm which had followed the King's acceptance of the Constitution the previous year her husband had been appointed Minister in Holland. Their arrival in the Hague had coincided with a round of balls and celebrations for the marriage of the Stadtholder's son to the Princess of Prussia, a circumstance, she wrote, that suited her twenty-one years to perfection. "I had brought with me many elegant toilettes from France, and soon became very much the fashion . . . I was dazzled by my success, little realising how short a time it was to endure."

In March 1792, with Dumouriez' appointment as Foreign Minister, her husband was dismissed from his post. For the time being however they remained in Holland, where they rented a small house and where Madame de la Tour du Pin, still fêted and spoiled, continued to be a leader of society. As the news from France grew more and more alarming, her husband left Holland, first for London, then to Paris, to look after his family affairs. In November a decree in the National Convention ordering all émigrés to return to France, or else face confiscation of their property, made it necessary for her to return as well. (Her assets in France included the freehold of the Swedish embassy in the rue du Bac, whence Madame de Staël had recently departed.)

Madame de la Tour du Pin set out from the Hague on December 1, with her two year old son, the nurse, and two servants. "Flattered as I had been in Holland," she wrote, "I still thought I had made the greatest sacrifices any one could require of me when I agreed to do without the services of my elegant maid and my footman-hairdresser. I realised, it is true, that I might not be able to have a carriage in Paris, that I might no longer go to balls, that I might even find myself obliged to spend the winter in the country but I resolved to bear these reverses with courage and determination."

Her journey took her through Antwerp which only that day had succumbed to the French army invading the Spanish Netherlands. She spent the night there, barricaded with the nurse and her child in their room at the inn, while outside the sky was lit with flames as the victorious army gave itself to pillaging and burning. By the time she arrived in France all easy illusions as to what lay ahead had vanished. "I had scarcely crossed the border when the Revolution was all about me, dark and menacing, laden with danger." She had left France as a light-hearted girl; now, looking back on her past life, she reproached herself for its futility.

"Some presentiment of other fates in store made me resolve very firmly to put away forever the thoughts of carefree youth, the far from disinterested flatteries of the world and the vain successes to which I had aspired. A bitter sadness gradually filled my heart as I realised the frivolity of the life I had led until then. Still, I felt that I possessed qualities which fitted me for more useful things, and so I was not discouraged, but felt rather that in such disastrous times I should refresh and strengthen the springs of my being. . . From that day forward, my life was different, my moral outlook was transformed."

She rejoined her husband in the little village of Passy, where the house he had taken was large enough for them to live in the back quarters, leaving all the windows on the street front shut, thus giving the impression that it was unoccupied. A local cabriolet, with a broken down horse, took them each day to Paris, where her father, General Arthur Dillon, was living in the Chaussée d'Antin. Dismissed from his post in the Revolutionary army, when, after August 10, he had called on his troops to renew their oath of loyalty to the King, he was now devoting his energies to rallying support on his behalf. He would pay for this loyalty later with his head. Meanwhile the trial of the King, and the question of its outcome, absorbed the attention of the country to the exclusion of all other subjects.

Chapter 10

From the safe haven of Switzerland Madame de Staël followed the news from France, and above all of the King, with growing anguish. The ideal of a constitutional monarchy was dead; the King's fate lay in the balance. Her father, no less distressed than she, was working on a pamphlet in the King's defence; its publication would lead to the sequestration of his assets in France. Narbonne, as the trial grew imminent, had written from England to the National Convention demanding a safe conduct to appear as a witness on the King's behalf. For Madame de Staël, who only a few days before had given birth to a son – "behold me mother of the Gracchi," she wrote to Gibbon – this chivalrous gesture was an act of treachery towards their love. In risking his life he threatened hers. "If you set foot in France," she announced dramatically, "I shall instantly blow out my brains." Narbonne's request was refused by the National Convention, and she breathed again. "Those tigers are more humane than you," she wrote next day.

Away from Madame de Staël, no longer swept along with her in the excitement of their shared political activity, Narbonne was beginning to find the extravagance of her devotion hard to bear. In letter after letter she assured him of her love, bombarding him with reproaches when he failed to reply, and losing no chance to remind him that he owed his life to her. The birth of her baby now made it possible for her to join him in his English exile – her two sons could be left behind in Switzerland. To the consternation of her parents, who did their utmost to prevent her, she began to make her preparations for the dangerous journey across Europe.

Narbonne awaited her arrival with resignation. His political hopes in ruins, consumed with anxiety for the King, his thoughts were with his monarch, not his mistress. Having failed to obtain a safe conduct to France he was engaged in composing his own defence of the King, with special reference to his period as Minister of War – the King, amongst other charges, was accused of hindering the army's preparations for war. In London he sought to rally political opinion to intervene to save the King, demanding and obtaining an interview with the Prime Minister. His pleas were icily received. "For no consideration in the world," said Pitt, "can England expose herself by pleading in vain on such a subject and before such men."

In France the King's appearance before the National Convention on December 11 to hear the charges made against him marked the opening of his trial. Despite the opposition of the Jacobins, he was allowed to choose counsel for his defence. The cowardice of the well-known advocate Target, who at the age of fifty-four pleaded that he was too old to undertake the task was balanced by the heroism of the aged former minister, Malesherbes, who courageously offered his services and who, with two others, was eventually assigned to the role.

Malesherbes' self-sacrificing offer, which would bring him to the guillotine the following year, met a generous and quixotic response from a wholly unexpected quarter. On December 15 a letter offering to share the burden of the King's defence was read out in the National Convention. Its author was Olympe de Gouges.

★   ★   ★

Olympe de Gouges, as we have seen, had begun the Revolution as a constitutional monarchist. The King's flight to Varennes had undermined her royalist sympathies; though she deplored the violence of August 10 she had welcomed the creation of a republic. Circumstances had changed but not her avid thirst for publicity nor her ardent sense that the Revolution owed women too the gift of freedom. "As long as nothing is done to raise the soul of women," she wrote, "as long as men are not large minded enough to occupy themselves seriously with women's glory, the state will never prosper."

In offering now to share in the defence of the King, Olympe de Gouges was once more speaking out for women and for their spiritual equality with men. "Let us leave aside the question of my sex," she wrote. "Women, too, are capable of generosity and heroism as the Revolution has demonstrated on more than one occasion. But I am a frank and loyal republican, without stain or reproach. . . . I may therefore undertake to plead this cause."

The King, she argued, was at fault as a king, but deprived of that forbidden title, he ceased to be guilty as a man. The sins of his ancestors had all been visited on him; despite this, without the corruption of his court he might perhaps have been a virtuous king. Alone of France's tyrants he had not surrounded himself with courtesans; his domestic morals had been pure. "He was weak; he let himself be deceived; he deceived us; he deceived himself. That, in a nutshell, is the case against him."

"Citizen President," she continued, "I shall not put forward here the arguments I have in his defence. I ask only to be admitted by the Convention and Louis Capet [Louis XVI] to assist an old man of nearly eighty [Malesherbes] in a painful task which seems to me worthy of all the courage and strength of a younger age. . . . My zeal may perhaps appear suspect to Louis Capet; his infamous courtiers have doubtless painted me to him as a cannibal thirsty for blood; but how glorious it is to undeceive an unhappy and defenceless man." She concluded with a plea for the King's life. "It is exile, not death that he deserves. The Romans won immortality by banishing their king; the English brought disgrace on themselves by executing Charles I."

Olympe de Gouges' letter, humane and moderate as it now appears, was dismissed without discussion by the National Convention. The Assembly, remarked a witty journalist, had accepted her request to disregard the question of her sex and passed on to the order of the day. Outside the Convention her offer, which she had printed and placarded through Paris, was greeted with a storm of ridicule. "Who does she think she is to meddle in such things," demanded the *Révolutions de Paris*; "why doesn't she knit trousers for our brave *sans-culottes* instead?" More dangerously, a few days later, she was threatened by an angry crowd who had gathered outside her lodgings in protest. Another woman might have hidden indoors; Olympe de Gouges came down to face them. Her coolness provoked the crowd still further; someone seized hold of her head, and pulling off her cap proceeded to play the part of auctioneer: "Who'll bid me fifteen sous for the head of Olympe de Gouges?" "My friend," she replied, with perfect tranquillity, "I'll bid you thirty and I demand the first refusal." The ugly moment passed in laughter, and she was able to escape unharmed.

In offering to defend the King, Olympe de Gouges had knowingly put her life at risk. "I am ready to die," she announced. "One of my republican plays is about to be performed. If, at what may be a moment of personal triumph, I am deprived of life, and if, after my death, respect for the law survives, my memory will be blessed and my murderers, once enlightened, will shed tears on my tomb." Throughout the autumn she had been playing with fire; she had placarded Paris, "even to the corridors of the National Convention", with posters denouncing Marat, Robespierre and their followers. Passionately opposed to any form of bloodshed – "the blood, even of the guilty," she wrote, "eternally defiles a revolution" – her sympathies were with the more moderate Girondins. It was their arguments she applauded from the galleries of the National Convention, as the fate of the King was being decided, while in a second open letter she once more pleaded for his life. "His guilty head once fallen will no more be of any use. It has cost us too dear already not to draw a real advantage from it."

Though all parties, the uncommitted Plain included, were agreed on the King's guilt, the Girondins, still wishing to save him, had hoped at first to put the question of his fate to the country as a whole. The Jacobins were opposed to a plebiscite. All-powerful in Paris, where the clubs and the Commune were behind them, they feared the strength of the Girondins' support in the provinces. The Girondins, unwilling to be accused of royalist sympathies, eventually allowed themselves to be overruled; in the end, out of cowardice or conviction, more than a third of them voted for the immediate execution of the King. On January 20 the King was summoned to hear his sentence; on January 21, with exemplary calm and courage, he mounted the scaffold in the Place de la Liberté.

That morning, recalled Madame de la Tour du Pin, the gates of Paris had been closed and orders given that no reply was to be made to those who asked why. It was all too easy to guess the reason, and looking out towards Paris from the windows of their house in Passy her husband and she listened in vain for the rattle of musketry which would indicate that an armed uprising to prevent the execution was taking place. "Alas! the deepest silence lay like a pall over the regicide city. At half past ten the gates were opened and the life of the city took up its normal course once more. A great nation had just stained its history with a crime for which the centuries would reproach it – yet not the smallest detail of the daily round had changed."

★ ★ ★

Early in January, despite the despairing pleas of her parents, Madame de Staël had set out to join Narbonne. War with England now seemed imminent. "The earth trembles on all sides," she wrote to Gibbon, "and if I do not hasten my departure an abyss will open between my friend and me." Pausing for a few days in Passy where she was the guest of Madame de la Tour du Pin, she crossed the Channel from Boulogne on January 20. By the time she arrived in Surrey where Narbonne, with a group of fellow exiles had rented a substantial country house, the news of the King's execution had reached England, sending shock waves of horror through the country and reducing her lover to prostration. Any joy in their first meeting was overwhelmed by his grief. "Alas," wrote Madame de Staël, "the pain you were feeling tore my heart. The expression on your face, the efforts you were making over yourself, all found a grievous echo in my soul. Forgive me for loving you so passionately that I see grief like happiness, in you alone."

For Narbonne and his fellow liberals, distress at the death of the King was compounded by the fear that their policies, by undermining the throne, had indirectly helped to bring it about. Madame de Staël, even at this moment of despair, never doubted the justness of their aims; for Narbonne the crisis of conscience would be profound. Political disillusion, as much as the persistence of her emotional demands, would eventually drive them apart. For the next few months, till the threats of her parents and the scandal her liaison was causing drove her back to Switzerland, Madame de Staël remained in Surrey by his side. Around her, drawn by the magnetism of her personality, gathered the friends and former colleagues who had fled to England after August 10. Ruined, exiled, uncertain of their future, they continued to delight in company and conversation. At Juniper Hall, the house Narbonne had rented, the talk had all the wit and brilliance of her salon in the rue du Bac, and Madame de Staël, against the darkening background of events in France, would look back on her time in England as "four months of happiness snatched from the shipwreck of my life".

Chapter 11

Though Madame Roland, like her husband, had opposed the execution of the King, she refused to waste emotion on his death. "He was quite impressive on the scaffold," she said later, "but he deserves no special credit for this; kings are trained for public appearances since childhood."

Not only had Roland voted against the death of the King, he had published a pamphlet calling for a referendum, and had threatened to dismiss from his ministry anyone who signed one of the numerous public petitions calling for his death. But the question of the trial was only one thread in the tangled skein of his personal and political preoccupations. As Minister of the Interior he had long since lost his grip. The stream of directives and propaganda which issued from his ministry bore no relation to the real problems he confronted: food shortages, the collapse of the economy, potential anarchy in Paris. It was a common charge against the Girondins that they preferred to write and talk than act; it was more than justified in Roland's case.

Vilified in the Jacobin press, he was attacked with equal violence in the National Convention. In December he had been accused with his wife of taking part in a royalist plot. Madame Roland's appearance at the bar of the National Assembly, the dignity and obvious sincerity of her replies, had routed her accusers, but on January 6, returning to the attack, Robespierre had denounced the "virtuous" Roland for misusing government funds, and by implication conniving with the enemy as well. Unwell, sick at heart, no longer confident of his wife's affection, Roland lacked the strength to struggle on. The death of the King was perhaps the final straw. On January 22, the day after his execution, he offered his

Madame de Staël, after Gérard.

Théroigne de Méricourt.

Madame de la Tour du Pin.

Olympe de Gouges.

Madame Roland.

"Club patriotique des femmes", 1793.

March of the women on Versailles.

Depart des Heroines de Paris pour Versailles le 5 Octobre 1789.

"Woman has the right to mount the scaffold...": Place de la Révolution, 1793, by Mettais.

Madame Tallien.

A Republican divorce: a contemporary view.

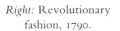

Right: Revolutionary
fashion, 1790.

Left: Post-Thermidoran
fashions, 1795:
"Merveilleuses et
Incroyable".

Joséphine de Beauharnais, by Prud'hon.

resignation as Minister of the Interior – the letter, save for a few small corrections, was entirely in his wife's firm hand. The Girondins, too weak and divided to support him, made no protest. Buzot, once his closest ally, remained silent.

Had the Rolands left Paris for the country after his resignation, they might have found some chance of safety. But Roland, obstinately determined to prove his honesty, had no intention of leaving till his accounts as a minister had been passed by the National Convention. The venal Danton might seek to cover his financial misdeeds with bluff and bluster, the virtuous Roland would prove he had nothing to hide. In this, as in all other political matters, he acted as one with his wife. Her husband's reputation was her own. The same ideal of virtue which made her resist her love for Buzot was one she carried through to public life. However narrow and misguided it might be – Madame Roland's refusal to make common cause with Danton is generally held to be one of the disasters of the Revolution – it was one that would sustain her through the nightmare months to come.

Already, fearing the worst, her husband and she had legally entrusted their daughter to her governess in the event of their imprisonment or death. While Roland meticulously cast and re-cast his accounts, the atmosphere around them grew more menacing each day. Attacks in the press continued, anonymous letters warned them of assassination attempts, sinister bands of *sans-culottes* gathered outside their flat. For a time they thought of moving or going into hiding; on one occasion Madame Roland went so far as to disguise herself in country-woman's clothes to leave the flat. The ruse disgusted her: a Girondin friend recalls her throwing off the plain bonnet she had just donned. "I am ashamed," she said, "to act like this. No, I shall neither disguise myself nor leave this place. If they want to murder me they must do it in my own house." It was a prospect which was rapidly becoming all too real.

★ ★ ★

On January 23, two days after the execution of the King, Olympe de Gouges' so called republican play, *L'Entrée de Dumourier* [sic] *à Bruxelles* had its first performance at the Théâtre de la République. Dumouriez was still a popular hero, aureoled with the glory of Valmy and Jemappes – Olympe de Gouges, like other playwrights of the day, was always ready to augment her fame by cashing in on that of others. In her present work Dumouriez, together with the young Duc de Chartres (son of Philippe Egalité) was a central character, with Dumouriez' army shown not only in a triumphant but a proselytising role – French soldiers fraternising with the citizens of Brussels to spread the message of the Revolution.

For Olympe de Gouges the choice of subject doubtless had a special meaning. Her only son, Pierre Aubry, child of a brief and unsuccessful marriage in her early youth, was an officer in Dumouriez' army. Now twenty-six, he was a somewhat unsatisfactory young man, who had already been in trouble with the authorities, but to Olympe de Gouges he was, as she declared, her only happiness on earth.

The play, despite its fashionably patriotic theme, was ill received. At the end of the evening as the leading actress came forward to announce the author's name, Olympe de Gouges leapt up from her box to forestall her. "It is I, Olympe de Gouges," she cried, "but if my play seems bad to you it is because it has been horribly ill acted!" This speech, not calculated to endear her to the actors, provoked a storm of hisses and derisive laughter, and in the confusion that followed, she was pursued by the audience into the corridors and narrowly escaped a mauling from the crowd. Undeterred, she returned for a second performance the next day. The evening was still more disastrous, with the audience invading the stage to dance the *Carmagnole*★ before the end, and thereafter the play was withdrawn.

Olympe de Gouges ascribed the failure of the play to the malice of those who disapproved of her offer to defend the King – "those wretches who reproach me for my lack of civic virtue because I

★A revolutionary dance and song.

thought his death was useless, and might be fatal to the republic" – and she denounced them vigorously in posters and her introduction to the play.

But if, in offering to defend the King, Olympe de Gouges had taken the first step towards her doom, her choice of Dumouriez as a hero would take her one stage further on the downward path. Less than two months later the French army, under his command, was crushingly defeated at Neerwinden. On April 5, having failed to rally his troops to march on Paris to overthrow the government, Dumouriez defected to the Austrians.

The news of his defection was a shattering blow to the Girondins. As Dumouriez' chief supporters they had reaped the glory of his victories; they now found themselves implicated, by association, in his guilt. In the National Convention the conflict between Girondins and Jacobins moved towards its final stages. Personal vendettas flared, fanned by the gutter press; Marat, the hero of the *sans-culottes*, redoubled his demands for "blood and heads". The Girondins' attempt to arraign him ended in fiasco; Marat, garlanded with flowers and carried shoulder high into the Convention, was triumphantly acquitted.

Olympe de Gouges had her own opinion of Marat; he was, she considered, an "abortion of mankind", and Robespierre no less sinister, a man who portrayed himself as incorruptible yet sought a personal dictatorship. But still cherishing the illusion that all parties could unite in the face of France's common enemies, she called on them in yet another pamphlet to forget their differences. No doubt the son she idolised was once more in her mind: "Look how the generous host of France's most brilliant youth fly to our frontiers, there to shed their pure and stainless blood. And for whom, great heavens? For the fatherland, and not to gratify your selfish passions and place another tyrant on the throne."

*　*　*

Olympe de Gouges' call for unity was echoed in almost similar terms by Théroigne de Méricourt. Since her participation in the events of August 10 she had remained virtually silent through the autumn – she was working, it was rumoured, on an account of her experiences as a prisoner of the Austrians. Though legend would once more cast her as a fury, she had played no part in the horrors of the September massacres. Her sympathies, like Olympe's, were with the Girondins; they were soon to prove her undoing.

In the spring of 1793, as the conflict between Jacobins and Girondins reached its final stage, she threw herself once more into the political fray with a pamphlet exhorting all parties to forget their quarrels. From her experiences in Austria, she wrote, she could confirm that patriots of all political complexions would be destroyed should the allies come to Paris. There was not a major figure in the political spectrum about whom she had not been questioned, and on whom vengeance would not be taken. On the grounds of self-interest, and still more on those of patriotism, the government should unite behind the army, demoralised by the spectacle of their divisions and dissensions.

She concluded with a final feminist proposal – far different from her call to arms the previous year – to set up committees of women in each Paris section, who, dressed with sashes emblazoned with the words "peace and friendship", would supervise the conduct of citizens in their quarter. The proposition, like so many previous initiatives, was ignored.

The days of such individual activists as Théroigne de Méricourt and Olympe de Gouges were coming to an end. Essentially their appeal had been to the middle classes though their own *déclassé* status had helped to work against them. They had never commanded an important following. But from the end of 1792 the feminist torch would be taken up by a new and more radical grouping. Women of the people, always an important element in the sporadic crowd scenes of the Revolution, were now beginning to demand a greater say in the political issues of the day, above all where questions of subsistence were concerned. In February 1793 they organised riots against the high cost of sugar, candles, and coffee, invading grocers' and chandlers' shops throughout the city, and forcibly reducing prices. The question of fixed, or maximum, prices was one which had divided Girondins and Jacobins, the Girondins essentially believers in a free market, the Jacobins ready to impose price controls with severe penalties for hoarders. In the struggle between the two parties, working class women were firmly on the side of the far Left, supporting and at times going further than the Jacobins. Their leaders had already identified themselves; Pauline Léon, a former chocolate maker, and Claire Lacombe, an actress who had reached Paris from the provinces in 1792 and who, like Théroigne, had earned herself a civic crown on August 10. It was with Pauline Léon as their president that in May 1793 they formed what would become the most famous of women's clubs in the Revolution, the Société des Républicaines-Révolutionnaires.

Avowedly committed to "frustrating the projects of the republic's enemies", the Républicaines-Révolutionnaires made their first headquarters in the library of the Jacobin Club. Their regulations were formal, with strict rules of procedure, an elected president, wearing a red cap of liberty, and sub-committees to deal with administration, correspondence and relief. But it was in the streets that their influence was felt most strongly. In the popular demonstrations that led to the downfall of the Girondins they were wholehearted supporters of the Jacobins, parading the streets in red woollen caps and red pantaloons, heckling and shouting down the Girondins at public meetings and from the galleries of the National Convention. On June 2, when the Jacobins, with the backing of the mob, forced the expulsion of twenty-nine Girondin deputies from the National Convention, they patrolled the doors of the building to prevent the escape of members leaving in protest. For the Girondins they were figures of horror; Buzot, in his memoirs, describes them as abandoned women, escaped from the gutter, "monstrous females with all the cruelty of weakness and all the vices of their sex". For Théroigne de Méricourt, who throughout her tempestuous career had consistently preached the emancipation of her sex, they would, ironically, prove the instruments of her destruction.

Her call for unity had been her swansong. Though not explicitly naming the Girondins, its plea for moderation had been Girondin in tone. A few days later, on May 15, she was attacked by a band of women outside the National Convention, who stripped her and flogged her brutally – such public floggings, humiliating their (generally female) victims, were a relatively common feature of mob justice. An entry in the *Courrier des Départements* two days later makes clear the political nature of the attack. "A heroine of the Revolution, the day before yesterday, experienced a little setback on the terrace of the Feuillants. Mademoiselle Théroigne, apparently, was recruiting women for the Roland faction; unfortunately she applied to devotees of Marat and Robespierre who, not wishing to increase the army of the Brissotins, seized hold of the female recruiter, and beat her with all the energy desirable. The guard arrived at last and rescued her from these indecent furies . . . *sic transit gloria mundi.*"

Théroigne de Méricourt had long shown signs of instability. Her sufferings in Austria, the violence of the experience of August 10, had all served to unsettle her reason. Half dead from her injuries, the flogging she had received dealt her the *coup de grâce*. She continued to operate lucidly for a while – a letter of July 1793 shows her dealing, quite rationally, with a financial matter – but by the spring of 1794, she had become insane. From 1795 till the end of her life in 1807, she would be confined in a lunatic asylum, still howling, wrote Michelet, with a certain romantic exaggeration, as she had done on the day she was attacked. "It was a sight to break one's heart," he wrote, "to see this charming and heroic creature fallen lower than a beast. . . . It pleased the royalists to regard it as God's vengeance on the woman whose fatal beauty had intoxicated the Revolution in its opening days."

Chapter 12

From the moment of Dumouriez' defeat at Neerwinden the Rolands had been increasingly at risk. Even before his defection Dumouriez had become a suspect figure; as a former fellow minister (however out of sympathy personally) Roland was linked by implication in his guilt. His attempts to prove his integrity as minister had failed miserably. Eight times he had petitioned the National Convention to examine his accounts; the assembly, playing cat and mouse, consistently postponed their examination, at the same time refusing him a passport to leave Paris till the matter had been cleared.

On March 31 his flat was searched, and his papers seized. Madame Roland, seeing the writing on the wall, and judging that her husband could escape from Paris more easily unencumbered by his family, decided to seek passports for her daughter and herself to leave for the country. She was inspired, she hinted in her memoirs, by another motive too: in leaving Paris she would leave behind her Buzot and the conflict between love and duty that had made life with her husband intolerable over the last few months.

Her passports were deliberately held up by hostile officials; by the time she at last received them, towards the end of May, she had fallen ill. A violent attack of "colic", the consequence perhaps of the nervous strain under which she had been living, confined her to bed for six days. When she was well enough to get up it was already too late. On May 31 the tocsin of the Hôtel de Ville sounded the general alarm. The gates of the city were closed. The Paris sections, committed to the Jacobin cause, had appointed a Revolutionary Committee whose aim, "to take and execute immediately all the measures necessary for the public safety it deems necessary", was in fact to overthrow the Girondins. Their first attempt was inconclusive; it was not until June 2, when the mob and the National Guard surrounded the Chamber, that the Convention, yielding to the threat of force, expelled the leading Girondin deputies, to place them, ostensibly, under house arrest.

But already on the 31st the Revolutionary Committee claimed the power to arrest private citizens. That evening, at about 5.30, a group of armed men arrived at Roland's flat with a warrant for his arrest. Roland protested vigorously – "I know of no law," he said, "which gives you the authority you claim, and I shall not comply with your orders. If you use violence I can only resist with the strength of my advanced years, but I shall protest to my last breath." The captain, unwilling to go further without fresh instructions, agreed to return to the Commune with his answer, leaving the rest of his men on guard outside.

Faced with the crisis she had long been dreading Madame Roland recovered all her former energy. Her appearance before the National Convention the previous December had been a personal triumph. A further intervention there might save her husband from arrest, or at least bring about his release. Pausing only to tell her husband of her plans, she quickly penned a letter to the President, then heavily veiled, with a black shawl slipped around her shoulders, she set out for the National Convention.

The courtyard outside the Tuileries was crowded with armed men, the doors to the Convention itself were all barred and guarded. After infinite difficulties she managed to bluff her way into a waiting room inside and to pass her letter to a friendly usher. An hour of anxious waiting passed. Pacing up and down, Madame Roland kept her eye fixed on the chamber from whence, whenever the door was opened, an indescribable tumult could be heard. The combat between Girondins and Jacobins was at its height. Realising at last that there was no chance of obtaining a hearing amidst such scenes, at least for the next hour or so, she decided to return home to discover what was happening. She flung herself into a cab. The horses seemed to move all too slowly, the streets were blocked at intervals by battalions of marching men. Paying off the cab, she made the last part of her journey on foot, arriving half fainting at her apartment where the proprietor of the building revived her with a glass of wine. From him she learnt the good news that Roland had managed to evade his guards and slip away through a back entrance. Guessing at his hiding place, Madame Roland sought him out at the apartment of a friend. But she was determined, despite all persuasions, to make her protest, and after a hurried interview she set out once more for the National Convention. She was never to see her husband again.

Great was her amazement on finding the courtyard of the Tuileries, so crowded before, was now almost empty; still worse was her disappointment on discovering that the session, which she had left in tumult, was over and the chamber deserted. The moment for her gesture was past – in the violence of the debates that day it had never really existed.

It was now late at night. Calling a cab, she directed it to the house of a friend with whom she was able to make plans for her husband's escape from Paris the next day, then refusing all offers to spend the night there, she set out for home.

"One may well ask why I returned to my apartment," she wrote later. It was not the place to go too deeply into her reasons, she explained, she could only describe her conclusions. Less important than Roland, she felt her arrest would be less likely; if it should take place she could use the occasion to plead her husband's cause and confound his opponents. Should the horrors of the prison massacres repeat themselves, it would prove that all was lost in Paris, and faced with the ruin of her country, she would rather die.

Even the thought of twelve year old Eudora did not give her pause. The child whom she had brought up in the full flush of Rousseauesque enthusiasm was proving a disappointment. "I have," she wrote, "an amiable daughter but unresponsive and indolent by nature. . . . She will be a good woman, with some talents; but her stagnant soul and tepid spirit will never bring me the joys I had promised myself. Her education can be completed without me; her existence will offer consolation to her father; but she will never experience my own lively feelings, neither my pleasures nor my pains." (Madame Roland did not always sustain this coolly distant attitude; her bitterest tears in prison were for her daughter.)

Armed with her high resolves, her courage wrought up by the events of the evening, she returned to her flat. She had just time to soothe her servants, to embrace her daughter and to start a letter to her husband when a knocking at the door announced the arrival of a new deputation from the Commune. They had come to find Roland. Madame Roland denied all knowledge of his whereabouts, and after a while they retired with an ill grace, leaving a sentry on the door and one in the street below. There was nothing more to be done, she decided, but to gather her forces for what was to come. For the moment she was overcome with exhaustion; she ate some supper, she finished her letter to her husband, instructing her faithful servant, Fleury, to deliver it next day, and went to bed.

An hour later, just after one in the morning, she was wakened by her maid; the men from the Commune had arrived with new warrants, this time for her arrest as well as her husband's. Resistance was useless. Her tearful household watched numbly as the justice of the peace put seals on her furniture and possessions – her piano, her clothes, the familiar objects of her daily life. At seven in the morning it was time to say goodbye to her daughter and her servants, enjoining them to calm. Outside the flat two bands of armed men lined the way to the carriage which was awaiting her, while a crowd of curious onlookers gathered round. As the carriage rolled away there were cries of "To the guillotine!" from women in the crowd.

She was taken to the prison of L'Abbaye, scene of some of the most horrifying of the September massacres. Here, since no cell was ready to receive her, she passed the day in a little bedroom in the concierge's flat. As the door was locked behind her, she recorded later, she sat down to collect her thoughts after the agitations of the previous twenty-four hours. It was impossible not to fear for her friends, her husband and her country; she waited impatiently for the day's newspapers, she listened eagerly to the noises from the street. On her own behalf, however, she felt strangely calm. She did not doubt her own courage, in her personal relations; whatever the strength of her love for Buzot, she had nothing for which to reproach herself. "I consecrated myself resolutely to my destiny," she wrote, "whatever it might be."

★ ★ ★

With the fall of the Girondins the reign of Terror in France began in earnest. Already in March and April respectively the Revolutionary Tribunal and the Committee of Public Safety which were to be its chief instruments had been set up. The Girondins, still in power when they were established, would be among their first victims.

Even at a distance of more than twenty years Madame de Staël, in her *Considérations sur la Révolution française*, could not bear to write of the events of that period in detail. "One does not know how to approach the fourteen months that followed the proscription of the Girondins," she wrote. "It seems that like Dante one descends from circle to circle, plunging ever deeper into the inferno. . . . One fears even to embark on such a story, so ineffaceable are the traces of blood it leaves on the imagination."

Madame de Staël had no liking for the Girondins, whose overthrow of the King had brought about the ruin of her friends and ended all hopes of a constitutional monarchy. But she never forgot the rule, essential, as she thought, in politics: that failing all else, one should choose the lesser of two evils, however far that party's viewpoint might be from one's own. Between the Girondins and the Jacobins, she had no doubt which to choose.

In the last days of May, whilst in Paris the Insurrectionary Committee were planning the final stages of their coup against the Girondins, Madame de Staël, weeping bitterly, had said farewell to Narbonne and set out on her way back to Switzerland. At every stage of her journey she wrote to her lover, whose arrival, she hoped, would shortly follow hers. In Switzerland she was reunited with her husband: diplomatic relations between Sweden and France had been temporarily suspended and he was awaiting developments whilst staying with his parents in law. He still seemed much in love with her, wrote Madame de Staël to Narbonne, and had been full of solicitude when she had briefly fallen ill. "M. de Staël is sublime with a thousand and one attentions, but he cannot understand that all the lemonade in the world cannot raise him to the level of my heart." But it was important financially that the marriage should continue; she needed the money for Narbonne, left virtually penniless by the Revolution. She had almost persuaded her husband, she wrote, to accept a permanent *ménage à trois*, though the thought of his continuous presence was a prospect she could hardly bear.

Counterpointing such domestic matters, and her vehement reproaches as Narbonne once again proved a reluctant correspondent, were echoes of the news from France, one shock succeeding another in her letters. Sainte Beuve, in a famous passage, describes her sojourn in Switzerland through the months of the Terror. "She passed the time," he wrote, "in the canton of Vaud, with her father and some refugee friends. . . . On the terrace of Coppet her most constant meditations contrasted the dazzling sunlight and the peace of nature with the horrors everywhere let loose by the hand of man. Her talent maintained a religious silence; from afar off were heard, muffled and thick as the beating of oars upon the lake, the measured strokes of the guillotine upon the scaffold. The state of oppression and anguish in which she remained during those terrible months only suffered her, in the intervals of her active devotion to others, to desire death for herself and to look forward to the end of the world and this lost human race."

Madame de Staël was indeed actively devoted to others during this period. Using her money, and the convenience of her husband's diplomatic status which enabled him to issue Swedish passports, she was able to arrange a series of rescues for friends fleeing the guillotine and to shelter them thereafter. "What happiness it is to save a fellow being's life!" she wrote later. "One can no longer believe that one's own existence is futile, one can no longer be weary of onself." But her talent was certainly not silent. The imminent trial of the Queen, still in prison in the Temple since her husband's death, inspired her to write and circulate a pamphlet pleading for her life. At the same time she was engaged on her first major work, *De l'Influence des Passions sur le Bonheur des Individus et des Nations*. Published three years later, it reflected the turbulent political passions of the day and something of her own emotions too. The elusive Narbonne was showing no signs of wishing to join her in Switzerland; amidst torrents of reproaches and threats of suicide the one-sided affair was coming to an end. Madame de Staël would not be slow in finding consolation – a handsome young Swede, Count Axel Ribbing, had already appeared on the horizon. But her chapter on love, based largely on her relationship with Narbonne, foreshadowed Byron's famous maxim in its sad conclusion: "Love is a woman's whole existence. It is only an episode in the lives of men."

Chapter 13

Madame Roland's great love Buzot had been among those Girondins who had evaded his sentence of house arrest after the coup of June 2, 1793. With a number of others he had made his way to Normandy, there to whip up resistance to the Mountain and march on Paris, as he put it, "to restore the Convention".

Buzot had left Paris reluctantly; when he knew that Madame Roland was in prison his first impulse had been to remain and share her fate. He had been persuaded by his friends that he would be more use fighting to reverse things from the provinces and in the first few weeks after his expulsion he had flung himself energetically into the task of rallying the Girondins.

Madame Roland was closely confined in the Abbaye, her protests to the authorities ignored, the concierge's bedroom exchanged for a cramped and grimy cell, the air fetid with the smells from a butcher's yard outside. But her situation was not altogether hopeless; it still seemed possible that the Jacobins would be overthrown, or that she at least would be released. Meanwhile, thanks to the goodwill of the supervisor of the Paris prisons, Jean Grandpré, whom her husband had appointed to the post, she was able to receive letters and visitors, and to communicate with friends outside. Always an excellent housekeeper, she made the best of her prison surroundings. A clean cloth covered the rickety table on which she kept her books and writing materials; there were flowers on her window sill; she cleaned her cell herself each day.

Sophie Grandchamp, in her memoirs of Madame Roland, gives a moving account of her first visit to her friend. For some reason she had fallen out with the Rolands during their period of power;

highly susceptible she had felt herself affronted by some real or imagined slight. But the news of Madame Roland's imprisonment brought her quickly to see her in prison. "My feelings on approaching the prison cannot be described," she wrote; " . . . the sound of the key in the lock made me almost faint." The tears rushed into her eyes as she greeted Madame Roland, and she lowered her head to hide them. It was only when she sat down next to her that she had the courage to look at her. Madame Roland had gone very red but showed no other sign of emotion at the meeting; her eyes were brilliant with an exhilaration which checked the words of sympathy on her lips. The two friends talked, Madame Roland telling her that she had begun to write notes on the recent political events; knowing that they would be destroyed if they were discovered, she asked Madame Grandchamp to take them for safe keeping – a perilous enterprise which she undertook with some alarm.

Through visitors such as Sophie Grandchamp, Madame Roland was able to hear news of her husband, her friends and above all of Buzot. His letters to her have been lost; by a strange fatality hers to him were discovered, amidst a bundle of old documents, on a second-hand bookstall in 1863. They were published, with considerable sensation the following year, the story of Madame Roland's love for Buzot, till then unknown or barely hinted at, revealed for the first time.

Her first letter, written to him on June 22, was full of her joy at having at last received one from him. "How often I reread it," she wrote. "I press it against my heart, I cover it with kisses, I had lost all hope of ever hearing from you again." The news that the Girondins had been arrested had filled her with despair; only when she heard of Buzot's escape and arrival in Normandy had she regained her calm. She urged him to continue his efforts there: "Brutus despaired too soon of the safety of Rome after the battle of Philippi."

As for herself, she could bear her captivity peacefully, while her only fear was that he might make some rash attempt to save her. Her daughter was safely with the family of a friend. Her husband, after twenty days of nerve-racking concealment in Paris, was now in hiding outside the capital. With these immediate anxieties behind her she could turn her thoughts entirely to her lover. To him alone she could confess that her arrest had been almost a relief. Her husband would be less ruthlessly pursued in consequence; should she herself be tried she hoped to acquit herself in a manner that would enhance his reputation. Above all she would be able to repay her husband for the pain she had caused him, yet be free of the burden of his presence. "Don't you see that in finding myself alone it is with you that I remain. Thus by my captivity I sacrifice myself for my husband, yet keep myself for you, and it is to my persecutors that I owe this reconciliation of love and duty: do not pity me!"

The efforts of the Girondins in Normandy to raise an army to march on Paris were meeting with little success. Taking Caen as their headquarters they issued proclamations denouncing the Jacobins, they made fiery speeches at public meetings, but their attempts to gather troops had failed for lack of volunteers. For the time being they remained at liberty, sheltered and lodged by the local authorities. But their movement was running out of impetus, whilst in Paris the central government, faced with outbreaks of revolt from more than twenty departments, was bending all its energies to resist them. In the Jacobin press denunciations of the Girondins reached a crescendo of ferocity, with Marat as ever leading the pack. It was Marat who, on June 2, had prepared the list of the deputies to be expelled; he had been the inspiration behind the mob who marched on the Convention that day. For the Girondins he was a monstrous figure; for one young woman, who had watched their arrival in Caen, first with excitement, then with growing disillusion, he was the chief author of her country's misfortunes. Her name was Marie-Charlotte Corday.

Daughter of a Norman family, impoverished but of noble stock, Charlotte Corday, like Madame Roland, had grown up steeped in the lofty ideals of Greek and Roman history. Now twenty-four, tall, well built, with something of the stature of a classical heroine, she was to put her ideals into practice.

On July 9, armed with a letter of introduction from the expelled Girondin, Charles Barbaroux, to a sympathetic deputy, Claude Lauze-Deperret, she set out for Paris. Her ostensible mission, to obtain the restoration of a pension for a friend, was unsuccessful. Her main objective, the death of Marat, was dramatically achieved. Her entry into his house, under the pretext of bringing him information about the Girondins in Caen, his promise to guillotine them all, the murderous knife thrust as he sat in his bath, were soon a sensation throughout France. Through her subsequent arrest and trial she maintained the calm of a heroine of antiquity, sustained by the words of her ancestor Corneille: "It is the crime, and not the scaffold that brings shame." She was executed on July 17.

"She has killed us," wrote the Girondin deputy Vergniaud, "but she has taught us how to die." Charlotte Corday's choice of Marat, already gravely ill from the skin disease for which he sought relief in his bath, had, in fact, been disastrous for the Girondin cause. It made Marat a martyr; it blackened the reputation of the Girondins in Caen, supposedly accomplices in the plot, rallying public opinion against them and hastening their eventual defeat. For Madame Roland too its consequences would be fatal. Charlotte Corday's contacts with Lauze-Deperret, whom she had seen twice during her brief stay in Paris, had led to his arrest the day after Marat's assassination. Amongst the letters found in his apartment were a number from Madame Roland to the Girondins in Normandy; it was on the basis of these that the prosecution would later found their case against her.

★　★　★

Marat's funeral procession the day before Charlotte Corday's death was conducted with a pomp and show of public emotion that made Madame Roland, when she heard of it in her prison cell, almost sick with rage. Four weeks later members of the Société des Républicaines-Révolutionnaires staged their own procession to honour his memory, adding their mite to the semi-hysterical worship of the dead hero – "*O cor Jesu, O cor Marat*" ★ – by swearing to bring up their children in the cult of Marat.

Perhaps, obscurely, they felt the need to redeem the reputation of their sex. Charlotte Corday's assassination of Marat had given rise to a wave of anti-feminism, confirming every masculine prejudice against women's emergence from the safe confines of home and family. As always in the daemonology of the time, sex, or the want of it, was seen to lie behind all female irruptions into public life. While figures such as Madame Roland, Olympe de Gouges and Marie Antoinette were commonly depicted as monsters of immorality and lust, Charlotte Corday was condemned for the reverse. After her death her body was taken to the Hôpital de la Charité where an autopsy was performed, in the presence of several doctors and a number of deputies, among them the painter David. "The monster was a virgin, virtuous with the virtue of women, that is to say chaste!" exclaimed a deputy; the fact was used as evidence of her lack of femininity. "This woman, who was said to be very pretty, was certainly not so," wrote an official newsheet. "She was a virago more brawny than fresh, graceless and dirty in her person as are almost all female philosophers and intellectuals. . . . Charlotte Corday was twenty-four, thus almost an old maid in our society, especially when her mannish build and bearing are taken into account. . . . She was a woman who had simply cast off her sex, experiencing only disgust and annoyance when nature recalled it to her. . . . Decent men do not like such women, and they in turn affect to despise the sex that despises them."

In the wake of Marat's death his journalistic mantle fell to the extremists of the day, the Enragés, for whom the policies of the Jacobins had begun to seem too tame. Claiming the *sans-culottes* as their followers they were also supported by the Républicaines – Révolutionnaires, who in July had broken away from the Jacobin Club to make their headquarters in the former church of Saint-Eustache. Both Pauline Léon and Claire Lacombe, the leading figures of the club, had liaisons with the Enragé journalist

★ "O sacred heart of Jesus, O sacred heart of Marat."

Théophile Leclerc, self-styled Friend of the People after Marat's death and founder of a paper of that name. He would later marry Pauline Léon.

It was Claire Lacombe, however, who attracted most attention from the public. Like Théroigne de Méricourt she had been awarded a civic crown for her part in the storming of the Tuileries; like her she demanded the right of women to bear arms. A ferocious enemy of the Girondins in the months leading up to their downfall she lost none of her revolutionary zeal thereafter. Her frequent interventions in the Jacobin Club and the National Assembly earned the indignant protest of one member: "That woman pushes herself into everything." "I doubt not," said another darkly, "that she is an agent of the counter-revolution."

The Républicaines-Révolutionnaires, with the Enragés, pressed for violent measures against hoarders and speculators – food shortages in Paris were becoming ever more acute – the control of prices, the stepping up of terror against all so called traitors and counter-revolutionaries. More political than feminist, they nonetheless demanded that the conditions of the new Constitution which offered universal male suffrage should be extended to women too. It was a purely formal demand, which expected and received no more than the promise that the question would be examined later. The new Constitution, presented to the Convention in June 1793, was in any case never to be implemented. Accepted with acclamation it was set aside for the duration of the war.

In July and August the Républicaines-Révolutionnaires could feel themselves to be at the height of their influence, freely accepted in the councils of the various Paris sections, a power to be reckoned with in the streets where their campaign to force women to wear revolutionary cockades in public resulted in a law to that effect. In fact their position had never been more precarious. The Jacobins, in a way that the Girondins had never been able to achieve, were tightening the reins of government. In the face of all-out war, with the enemy breaching their frontiers, with Toulon in the hands of the British, with the Vendée and half of France in revolt, they were in no mood to tolerate dissenters in the capital. The mob which had brought them into power was potentially an anarchic force; the radical demands of the Enragés threatened the interests of the bourgeois- or property-owning elements whose support they still needed. In their campaign to bring the Enragés under control, the Républicaines-Révolutionnaires and the vociferous women who swelled the mob would be among the first to be suppressed.

★ ★ ★

"O my poor sex," Olympe de Gouges had written in the previous year, "O women who have gained nothing from the Revolution." With the shelving of the Constitution all hopes of political rights for women had finally been put aside. But the Revolution had brought them other gains. Already under the Constituent Assembly women had been granted equal rights with men in family inheritances and the right to testify in legal matters. In September 1792, a more spectacular reform, divorce, had been made legal on equal terms for men and women – the grounds included incompatibility, mutual consent, the abandonment of one spouse by another for a period of two years. Though the law in practice favoured men – few women had the economic power to leave their husbands – at least an attempt at equal treatment had been made. Clubs for divorcees were formed, republican divorces, like republican weddings, were the subject of popular prints and engravings. More than three thousand couples, in Paris alone, availed themselves of this new law in the first year.

Olympe de Gouges could only welcome the law on divorce; her views on marriage, "the tomb of trust and love", were always jaundiced. But the right of women to express themselves politically remained, in her eyes, the one on which all others must depend. She condemned Charlotte Corday's action roundly, but she saw it as the natural consequence of excluding women from all part in public life. "In closing the doors of honour, employment and fortune to women," she wrote, "you compel them, as it were, to open those of crime."

Far from falling discreetly silent in the atmosphere of increased repression which followed Marat's death, Olympe de Gouges was still actively engaged in political journalism. With a courage verging on folly, she had sprung to the defence of the proscribed Girondins, declaring in a letter to the National Convention her readiness to share their fate. Now, three days after Charlotte Corday's death, she had published a new broadsheet, *Les Trois Urnes*, in which with even greater rashness she proposed a national plebiscite to solve the country's problems – the three urns of the title offering the choice, respectively, of "Republican government, one and indivisible", "Federal government", and "Monarchy".

It was a proposal not only dangerous but out of date. Since Louis XVI's death the idea of a monarchy had been unthinkable to all sections of opinion in the National Convention. The federal solution, dear to the Girondins, was anathema to the Jacobins – the crime of pursuing "federalism" would be one of the chief charges against the Girondins when they came to trial. Even to suggest that there was a choice, in the mood of the time, could be regarded as treason.

The last few days in Paris had been hot and torrid with frequent showers – Charlotte Corday's execution had taken place in the pouring rain. When Olympe de Gouges called on the bill poster who had promised to put up copies of her broadsheet round the town she was told that the weather was too bad to undertake the task. Unsuspecting and accompanied by her printer, she set out on the quest for someone else to do the job. She had just met up with a travelling salesman near the Pont Saint-Michel who agreed to take it on when two police commissioners, with a group of National Guardsmen, approached them and called on them to halt. The original bill poster, alarmed by the contents of her notice, had reported her to the authorities. After questioning, the salesman and the printer were released. Olympe de Gouges remained in custody. A week later, after her apartment had been searched and a number of documents seized, she was transferred to the prison of L'Abbaye.

Even in L'Abbaye, with daily news of political arrests, Olympe de Gouges refused to let herself be silenced. In a series of protests smuggled from her prison cell she denounced her persecutors, reserving her strongest invective for Robespierre and the Jacobin Club – "that infernal cavern whence the Furies vomit up their flood of poison and discord". It was Robespierre's hidden influence, she wrote, which had led to her arrest and, with superb disregard for the consequences, she accused him yet again of seeking a dictatorship. But it was her fate as ever to call out to deaf ears. If the Committee of Public Safety paid good heed to her remarks – it is amazing that she survived for the next three months – the general public heard her with complete indifference. A police report of September, when a new set of her placards had appeared, described the usual reaction to her posters. "People stop a moment, then walk off saying, 'Ah, it's only Olympe de Gouges'."

Chapter 14

On August 1 the widowed Marie Antoinette was moved from the Temple to the prison of the Conciergerie. In the struggle to the death against the invading enemy her trial would be a symbol of France's determination not to compromise with Austria or the allied powers. On August 23, giving concrete expression to that determination, the *levée en masse*, putting all of France's manhood at the service of the war, was declared.

Uniting equally against the enemy within, the Jacobin government stepped up their campaign against the Girondins expelled from the Convention, almost all now in prison or on the run. Troops and deputies were sent to bring dissenting towns to heel, amongst them Caen where at the end of July the Girondins who had made their headquarters there found themselves placarded as outlaws and forced to flee. In the royalist Vendée, where the Revolution faced outright civil war, a campaign of devastation was pursued.

On September 5, under pressure from the *sans-culottes* who in their last great coup of the Revolution besieged the National Convention, terror was proclaimed the "order of the day". On September 17 the terrifying Law of Suspects was passed, defining suspected persons in terms so vague and sweeping that almost no one, from then on, could count themselves safe from arrest.

Amongst the categories listed under this new law were "former nobles, their husbands, wives, fathers, mothers, sons, daughters, brothers or sisters . . . who have not constantly demonstrated their loyalty to the Revolution". It was a category into which Joséphine de Beauharnais, despite her carefully cultivated contacts, now found herself in danger of falling.

Till July her former husband's republican credentials would have been enough to shield her. From Chief of Staff to the Army of the Rhine he had been appointed its commander, creating such an excellent impression by his patriotic letters to the National Convention that at one point it was suggested he should become Minister of War. But his stirring letters hid a total inability to act, and his failure to relieve the French-held town of Mainz, which fell to the besieging Prussians in July, put an end to any credit he had previously enjoyed. He resigned his post in August, narrowly escaping arrest, and retired to his country estate.

With her husband's resignation there was no longer anything to keep Joséphine in Paris where, till then, she had discreetly pushed his interests with her friends in the National Convention. In any case, the atmosphere in the capital was now distinctly threatening, and since the Law of Suspects required all citizens to sign a declaration of citizenship based on residence she decided to leave Paris for the village of Croissy, ten miles outside.

In this peaceful backwater, relatively untouched by the fanaticism of the time, she signed herself in as a resident, renting a house in the main street of the village, with a view of trees and garden and the distant Seine behind. Her twelve year old son Eugène came to join her from Strasbourg where he had been staying with his father. His ten year old sister, Hortense, was already living with her mother and to avoid any taint of privilege had been apprenticed as a seamstress in the village. Eugène, on his arrival, was set to learn the trade of carpenter. Apart from these concessions to *sans-culotte* opinion Joséphine for a time was able to lead a comparatively normal life, dining quietly with neighbours and avoiding Paris as much as possible. A playmate of Hortense's recalls her at this time, thirty years old, slender and elegant, with delicate features and great sweetness of expression. "La Fontaine's line," she wrote, "could never have been more aptly applied than to her: '*Et la grâce, plus belle encore que la beauté*'."

Throughout the autumn, Joséphine remained in Croissy, unnoticed and unscathed. Meanwhile on his country estate, Alexandre de Beauharnais devoted himself to "projects for the good of the

Republic". Elected mayor of his local village he busied himself with patriotic speeches and committees, collecting testimonials to his patriotic zeal and hoping vainly that away from Paris and its dramas he might be able to ride out the storm.

* * *

For Madame Roland autumn opened in a sombre mood. From the end of August it had been clear that the Girondin cause was lost. Victims of their own indecision, they had allowed the weeks to slip away while the government in Paris, using terror as an instrument, consolidated its position. Her early hopes of confounding her opponents and influencing opinion in a dramatic public trial had faded. Her opponents had no intention of giving her such an opportunity.

On June 24, by a cruel trick, she had been released from l'Abbaye only to be re-arrested that same day and transferred to the prison of Sainte-Pélagie. The authorities, conscious that her first arrest by the Commune had been irregular, had arranged to re-arrest her in due legal form. She was charged with having aided and abetted her husband in stirring up federalism and in conspiracy to treason.

Sainte-Pélagie had originally been a prison for thieves and prostitutes, who still formed a large proportion of its population. Madame Roland's cell, little more than a cubicle, was one of many along a narrow corridor. Each morning the cell doors were opened by a gaoler with a heavy key, and their inhabitants could debouch along the corridor to a little courtyard or a dark and evil smelling room which served as meeting places. Madame Roland regarded most of her fellow prisoners with horror, recoiling from their conversation, and shocked still further by their shameless gestures as they called through the windows to the prisoners in the men's wing opposite. "So this is the place," she wrote indignantly, "reserved for the respectable wife of an honourable man. If this is the price of virtue on earth, let no one be astonished at my scorn for life, and the resignation with which I face my death."

But it was not in her character to let circumstances defeat her. To the violence of her indignation succeeded a stoical self-possession. She kept to her cell, stopping her ears to the obscenities and curses that reached her through the thin plaster walls. She still had her books, her writing materials and portrait of Buzot in the locket she wore close to her heart. She had always steadfastly refused to write for publication. Now, with posterity for her audience, all the pent-up feelings and experiences of her past found expression as with steady and unhurried hand she set herself to write her memoirs. Nourished on Rousseau, it was his autobiography she took as her model as she painted the scenes of her childhood and youth and even, with Rousseauesque frankness, described her first encounter with sex. So unpleasant had been the experience (an attempted seduction by her father's apprentice) that she had averted her mind from the subject for years after; her first night with Roland, she wrote, had been as surprising as it was unenjoyable. But it was on her early years, before her mother's death when she was twelve, that she dwelt most lovingly – years of tranquillity and affection "resembling those beautiful spring mornings when the serenity of the sky, the purity of the air, the brilliance of the foliage, the scent of plants give enchantment to everything that breathes". To recall them in her prison cell was to live them for a second time.

Parallel to her memoirs, with their memories of happier days, was an account of the political happenings of the previous few years, from her arrival in Paris to her present imprisonment. With passion and bias she drew the portraits of her political friends and enemies, untroubled even now by any thought that her own conduct had been mistaken, or that the Girondins by urging on the war, and their weakness in pursuing it, had opened the way for the stronger and more determined Jacobins. Nor did it occur to her that Roland, the pedantic civil servant, had been the victim of her ambition – without her driving thirst for action they might never have returned to Paris for the second time. Now in hiding with two spinster sisters in Rouen, Roland, she wrote to Buzot, had fallen into a state of total demoralisation and despair. Gnawed by jealousy of Buzot, he too had written his memoirs, so bitter in their description of his former colleague, that she had persuaded him to withdraw them.

The goodwill of the prison inspector, Grandpré, brought a temporary amelioration to Madame Roland's conditions of imprisonment. A room was found for her next to the concierge's, spacious enough for her to send for her piano and to study painting with the devoted Madame Grandchamp. But the improvement was shortlived. A few weeks later Grandpré was arrested, and Madame Roland was returned once more to her prison cell where, besides the prostitutes who had been her neighbours, there was now a new influx of political detainees. The Law of Suspects was beginning to take hold.

Madame Roland's last letter to Buzot – or the last that has survived – was written in the virtual certainty that she would not see him again. At the end of July he had been declared an outlaw and his house at Evreux razed to the ground. Forced by the approach of government troops to flee from Normandy, he had made his way with a group of fellow Girondins to Brittany, only to find that there too the Jacobins were in control. Here for a month he remained in hiding while a number of his companions set out towards Bordeaux, the homeland of the Girondins, and still, as they hoped, sympathetic to the Girondin cause.

Madame Roland saw no hope in Bordeaux; her eyes were fixed on America, where Buzot might yet find safety and a new life. In veiled terms, for she no longer dared write freely, she urged him to set out there; the knowledge that he was safe would be her greatest consolation. As for herself, she was prepared for whatever might happen, sustained by his love, by his letters and his portrait, over which she had so often wept.

But Buzot could not bring himself to leave France, and to distance himself perhaps for ever from Madame Roland. Even now, with Bordeaux and the south-west behind them, it might be possible to raise the country in revolt against the Jacobins. On September 20, with five other former deputies, he set out by boat from Brest for Bordeaux; they landed in the estuary of the Gironde four days later.

* * *

For others beside Buzot, Bordeaux, with its Girondin sympathies, had seemed to offer refuge. Thérésia de Fontenay, fleeing Paris, had made her way there earlier that year – availing herself before she did so of the new law that made divorce a possibility. Her husband had left for exile in the West Indies; she herself, twenty years old and freed from the yoke of an unsatisfactory marriage, was ready to plunge herself into whatever pleasures she could find. She passed the summer in a sense of false security, absorbed in various love affairs. The downfall of the Girondins had rallied Bordeaux against the central government; they planned to set up some kind of federal state with their neighbouring departments to ensure their independence. But their discussions were hopelessly disordered; while they debated ways and means the Revolutionary government was already on its way to crush dissent.

Madame de la Tour du Pin, like Madame de Fontenay, had seen Bordeaux as her best hope of safety. Heavily pregnant, she had taken refuge with a friend a little way outside the town. Her husband, after discussions with the federalist leaders there, had returned disgusted by their lack of urgency or organisation. By early September government troops had made their headquarters at La Réole, some thirty miles from Bordeaux, and by cutting off supplies of grain were able to put the city virtually under siege. The prospect of famine, and the threatening presence of the troops so near, were enough to undermine the resolution of the municipality. On September 18 the moderate council was overthrown, and a newly elected council had entered into negotiations with the commissioners of the National Convention at La Réole. Buzot and his companions had arrived in the Gironde just in time to put their heads into the noose.

Their story for the next few weeks would be one of increasing desperation and despair. Their arrival had been reported; hunted and on the run, they wandered miserably from hiding place to hiding place, sleeping in woods and ditches, a source of danger to anyone who helped them. They were finally taken in by a courageous friend, whose house in Saint Emilion had a cellar in the garden, where in damp and semi-darkness they were able to find a temporary refuge, unconsoled by any ray of hope in the news that reached them from outside. On October 16 government troops marched into Bordeaux, completing the Jacobin subjection of the Gironde. In Paris, a week later, the trial of Brissot and twenty fellow Girondins – "*les vingt et un*" – began, with its verdict a foregone conclusion from the first.

Chapter 15

The month that would end with the trial of the Girondins had begun with another, equally dramatic in the eyes of watching Europe; the trial of Marie Antoinette. As "*la louve Autrichienne*", the Austrian she-wolf, she had become the focus of the fears and hatreds of the embattled Revolution. Far more than her husband, at the time when they still had power, she had resisted the new order, remaining in communication with the Austrian court throughout the early stages of the war. The fear that should the monarchy be restored she might become regent for her son was a powerful sub-conscious factor in the anti-feminism of the time; should women be granted political power the Queen too might have a claim to rule. Hated and vilified, subjected to every kind of sexual smear, she had been made a monster in the nation's eyes. Now, with the National Convention too deeply committed to the war to use her as a possible hostage in negotiating a peace, the time for a final decisive gesture, cutting all links with the pre-revolutionary past, had come.

Today, whatever one's political viewpoint, it is impossible to read the account of her trial and final days without emotion. Her courage and dignity in the midst of degradation – with a guard in constant attendance in her prison cell, "even on occasions of nature", racked by haemorrhages, accused in court of incest with her son – raised her to a level that approaches the sublime. Her last letter to her sister-in-law, full of resignation and forgiveness, would be read in the churches of France through most of the nineteenth century. On October 16, a white-haired old woman at the age of thirty-seven, she made the journey through the Paris streets to the guillotine.

Madame Roland was one year older than the Queen and like her had suffered the anguish of separation from her child. (Elizabeth, the Queen's daughter, would survive the Revolution. The little Dauphin died in 1796.) But even now, in the shadow of approaching death, she could show no sympathy towards her. Her hatred of royalty, and of the Queen in particular, was too deeply engrained, and it is disconcerting to read, in a letter to Robespierre, of her indignation that she, a patriot, who had sacrificed herself to the utmost for her country, should be punished equally with "the arrogant and shallow minded woman who curses the name of equality".

The letter to Robespierre, written in the hope that he would vindicate her husband, his former friend and colleague, was never sent. She had sought no pity for herself; after twenty-four hours of reflection she came to recognise the uselessness of seeking it for others. "Once my letter can have no effect, it is out of place," she wrote; "it can only compromise me uselessly with a man who may destroy me but cannot debase me." Her political memoirs gave her final verdict on the man she had once so admired. "This Robespierre, whom I thought an honest man, is an utterly atrocious being. How he lies to his conscience! And how he loves blood!"

The news of the approaching trial of the Girondins, wrote Sophie Grandchamp, reduced Madame Roland to such a state of agitation that for a while she tried to keep all information from her for fear that she might attempt to commit suicide. In fact, the idea of suicide had already entered Madame Roland's mind. Her first thought was to starve herself to death, and in a farewell letter, written on October 3, she made her *adieux* to those she loved, her husband, her daughter, her faithful maid, and then, in a paragraph which her literary editors suppressed for more than fifty years, to Buzot. "And you, whom I dare not name," she wrote, " . . . you who respected the barriers of virtue despite an overwhelming passion, will you grieve at seeing me precede you to those realms where we may love each other without crime; where nothing will prevent our being united? . . . I go there to await you; to remain on earth as long as virtue has a refuge to denounce the injustice which condemns you. But if relentless misfortune dogs your steps, do not suffer a mercenary hand to strike you, die free as you have lived." Eight months later, rather than face arrest in the cellar where he had hidden, Buzot would stab himself to death.

But Madame Roland, though she fasted long enough to be transferred to the prison infirmary, put aside her resolution for a while. She no longer had any hope of freedom but she could yet preserve herself to bear witness for her friends as they faced their travesty of a trial. Summoned to testify at the opening session on October 24, Madame Roland was brought from her prison to the Palais de Justice to hear the charges against the twenty-one, then put on one side in the office of the Clerk of the Courts, to wait to be called. The summons never came, and for five days she was on tenterhooks, while she worked on a statement in their defence. On October 30 the trial of the Girondins was brusquely brought to an end, no further witnesses being considered necessary, and the sentence of death pronounced on them all. They went to the scaffold the next morning.

To Madame Grandchamp fell the harrowing task of breaking the news to Madame Roland. "I dragged myself to La Pélagie," she wrote, "my face and my expression dispensed me of any need to announce the crime. On hearing my voice my friend got up to greet me; scarcely had she seen me than she fell back, sinking down on her chair; the pallor of death covered her face, my tears called her back to life; her own began to flow, relieving her. 'It is for my country,' she told me, 'that I shed these tears: my friends are dead as martyrs for liberty; their memory requires no mark of weakness. Now my destiny is fixed; I no longer have any uncertainty, in a little while I shall rejoin them and I shall show myself worthy to follow in their footsteps.'"

That same afternoon, Madame Roland was transferred to the Conciergerie, the prison which had been the ante-chamber to the guillotine for both Marie Antoinette and the Girondins – the Palais de Justice, where the Revolutionary Tribunal held its sessions, was part of the same building. If conditions had been bad in Sainte

Pélagie, they were infinitely worse in the Conciergerie. Grossly overcrowded, dark, foul smelling, its walls sweating with damp from the nearby Seine, it housed more than three hundred prisoners of both sexes. For most, a bed of filthy straw was all that was provided, though Madame Roland, through the kindness of a fellow prisoner had a mattress and was given a cell to herself. She had no more than eight days to live but during that time she created an indelible impression on all those with whom she came in contact.

We see her, for instance, through the eyes of the Comte Beugnot, one of the few prisoners to survive the Conciergerie where the average life expectation in the Terror was a matter of weeks or even days. Himself a royalist, he had certainly no bias in her favour, and her political opinions, expressed with great passion and vigour, amazed him by their boldness and intolerance. "She would allow no talent, uprightness, virtue or enlightenment except in Roland and his admirers; everywhere else she would see only baseness, ignorance and treason." But separated from her political views, she appeared quite otherwise. With her eloquent and gentle voice, her obvious emotion when she spoke of her husband and child, she seemed the image of an ideal wife and mother, happiest of all in the midst of her domestic duties.

"I must add too, to her credit," he wrote, "that she established an ascendancy highly honourable to herself, even in the depths of the dungeons. On the same straw and behind the same locks were flung indifferently the Duchesse de Grammont and a stealer of handkerchiefs, Madame Roland and a street walker, a nun and a madwoman. For refined women this mixture had the cruelty of forcing them to watch a daily spectacle of horrible and disgusting scenes. We were woken each night by the shrieks of fallen women, tearing each other to pieces. Madame Roland's cell was an island of peace in the midst of this hell. If she descended into the courtyard, her very presence created order, and these unhappy creatures, whom no force could control, restrained themselves for fear of displeasing her. She gave money to the neediest among them, advice, consolation and hope to all."

Serene and courageous in public, her spirits sometimes failed in private. "She gathers all her strength in front of you," a woman prisoner told another witness, the Girondin Jean Riouffe, "but sometimes she weeps for three hours on end, leaning up against the window in her cell."

On November 1 Madame Roland went for the first of two interrogations before her trial. Insulted and alternately harried and interrupted by her questioners, she remained cool enough to write a detailed account of both proceedings which tallied in almost every particular with the official record. With her letters to Lauze Deperret establishing a link with the Girondins in Normandy, she could be accused of conspiring with them as well as having, through her husband, corrupted public opinion during his period as Minister of the Interior. Denying all such accusations, she refused point blank to answer any question as to her husband's whereabouts. "I know of no law," she announced, "in the name of which one is obliged to betray the dearest sentiments of nature."

But she cherished few hopes for her husband. To Beugnot, astonished by her icy resolution, she said, "If I had been free, and my husband conducted to his execution, I would have stabbed myself at the foot of the scaffold, and I know that when Roland hears of my death he will kill himself." It was for her daughter that she felt the greatest pangs. Since the trial of the Girondins it had been too dangerous for her to remain with the family to whom she had been first entrusted, and she had been entered in a boarding school under an assumed name. Madame Roland's final letter, written on the day before her trial, was to the headmistress of the school, signed simply, since her own name could only be a danger, "the mother of Eudora". "It is easy to bear ones own misfortunes," she wrote, "but it is difficult to calm a mother's heart on the fate of a child from whom she is to be torn away," and in a brief and touching letter, all the more moving for its lack of emphasis, she commended her daughter to her care.

On November 8 Madame Roland went to face her trial, mounting the stairs that led from the cells below to the great vaulted chamber that was the seat of the Revolutionary Tribunal. She had dressed herself with care, recalled Comte Beugnot, who came to talk to her beside the grille that separated the women's quarters from the men's as she waited for the moment to be called. She was wearing a dress of white muslin with a black velvet sash; beneath a simple bonnet her long hair flowed about her shoulders. Her face seemed more animated than usual; there was a smile on her lips though all those round her were in tears. When the call to the Tribunal came, she turned to Beugnot and squeezed his hand. "Farewell monsieur," she said, "let us make peace; it is time to do so." Lifting her eyes to his she saw that he was fighting back his tears, a prey to violent emotion. She seemed touched, but added only two words more: "Have courage."

Beneath a statue of Justice in the midst of the hall sat the five judges of the Revolutionary Tribunal, each dressed in black with a tricolour sash and the tall hat plumed with ostrich feathers that were the uniform of their office. Madame Roland took her seat on the bench of the accused on one side of the hall, facing the jury on the other. The proceedings began with the questioning of other witnesses; her manservant, Fleury, her faithful *bonne*, and the governess Mademoiselle Mignot. While the manservant and Fleury stoutly denied any suggestion that their mistress was involved in a conspiracy – for which the first would pay with his head, the second by imprisonment – the governess did her best, in a series of venomous innuendoes, to imply that the Rolands were in the enemy's pay. Her evidence, even in that setting, was too flimsy to be accepted; in any case it was unnecessary. The letters to Lauze Deperret were enough to seal Madame Roland's fate. Her efforts to defend herself, and to justify her husband and the Girondins, were brutally cut short. She was sentenced to be executed that same day.

She returned from her condemnation, wrote a fellow prisoner, with a hasty, almost joyous step, indicating by an expressive gesture the way the judgement had gone. There was just time for her to eat lunch which she shared with another prospective victim, a terrified forger of government bonds, whom she rallied into eating with jokes and kindly words. The prison barber came to cut their hair. She watched her own long locks fall to the floor, and congratulated her companion on his Roman looks when his hair too was shorn.

The execution was timed for mid-afternoon. Arms tied behind her back she mounted the tumbril, leaning against one end of the cart to remain firmly upright as they made the hour-long journey to the Place de la Révolution (now the Place de la Concorde) where the guillotine was mounted. There were few people watching the procession; the day was cold and wintry, too cold to linger outside; famine and the daily struggle for existence had diverted attention from what had become an increasingly familiar spectacle. But at the corner of the Pont Neuf, almost lifeless with emotion, stood Madame Grandchamp. It had been Madame Roland's last request that she would stand at that spot to watch her as she went to her death.

As the cart drew near the place where she was standing there was cries of "*la voilà, la voilà*", from the little knot of spectators gathered there. Fixing her eyes on the figure in white, Madame Grandchamp watched the procession's slow approach. Madame Roland, she wrote, was "fresh, calm, smiling", a total contrast to her abject companion whom from time to time she tried to cheer. On reaching the bridge her eyes searched the crowd for the face of her friend; a smile and a look showed her satisfaction that she had not failed her at this final rendezvous. Fighting her emotion, Madame Grandchamp managed to remain standing till the tumbril had disappeared into the distance, then, overcome by the violence of her feelings, she all but collapsed; she never knew afterwards how she found her way home.

In the centre of the Place de la Révolution stood a vast plaster statue representing Liberty – the work of the artist Jacques Louis David, it had been erected that summer to celebrate the anniversary of August 10. The guillotine stood further along the square, a gaunt silhouette against the November sky, with a cordon of soldiers at its foot. Here at least a considerable crowd had gathered, with the inevitable *tricoteuses* to the fore. There were chairs for hire for those who wished to watch the spectacle in comfort. Lemonade sellers and news vendors hawked their wares amongst the spectators. The tumbril drew up, the victims descended. Madame Roland faced the insults which were shouted at her with an ironic smile. Thoughtful even now for her terrified companion, she asked that he should be executed first in order to spare him the spectacle of her death. Sanson, the executioner, demurred. "Surely," she said, smilingly, "you won't refuse a lady's last request?" and after a moment's hesitation he agreed.

Unflinching, she watched her companion's death, then in her turn she mounted the short ladder to the platform. As she raised her eyes to David's statue across the sea of watching heads she uttered her famous apostrophe: "O Liberty, what crimes are committed in thy name." A few seconds later she was strapped to the plank. The blade fell. Her body and that of her companion were bundled into a cart and taken to the cemetry of La Madeleine where they were flung in the same ditch. "Better to kill the devil than be killed," wrote Hébert gaily in the *Père Duchesne*; " . . . the *sans-culottes* have done well, Dame Coco, to catch you red handed; for if your old cuckold of a husband hadn't fallen flat on his face with his *brissotage*, you'd have been a second Austrian."

A visitor brought the news of her mother's death to Eudora's boarding school. Knowing that the slightest sign of emotion might betray her hostess and lead to her destruction, the child had the courage to restrain her tears till she could break down alone. Madame Roland, wrote a friend, could have been proud of her daughter that day. As for Roland, when he heard that his wife had been sentenced to death, he determined, as she had prophesied, to kill himself. He had two possible courses, either to give himself up and to use his trial to denounce the crimes of the regime, or to put an end to his days himself. He decided on the second course, since should he be tried and arrested, his goods, and hence Eudora's inheritance, would be sequestrated. On the evening of November 10, refusing to listen to the pleas of the two sisters who had sheltered him, he left Rouen on foot and set out into the countryside. Four miles outside the town he stopped beneath the trees by the side of a lane and stabbed himself twice with a swordstick. His body was found the next morning with a note:

"Not out of fear but indignation. I left my refuge at the moment I heard my wife was to be murdered; I no longer wish to remain in a world so steeped in crime."

★　★　★

Five days before the death of Madame Roland, Olympe de Gouges had made her way to the scaffold. Shivering in the chilly November rain which fell steadily that afternoon, she had wept on the long journey to the Place de la Révolution, though from time to time she had rallied her spirits to talk of politics with feverish animation. At the sight of the guillotine she collapsed entirely, and only at the final moment, as the executioner prepared to strap her to the plank, did she recover her voice. "Citizens," she cried, "you will avenge my death."

Till almost the last moment, it had seemed impossible to Olympe de Gouges that she would be found guilty of any offence against the State. Transferred earlier to an infirmary "for those whose health has undergone some alteration", she could even, had she wished, have taken the opportunity to escape; security was lax and a sum of money could have ensured her freedom. She had refused the opportunity, certain that a trial would vindicate her. It was only at the end of October, when she was transferred to the Conciergerie that she realised the uselessness of her illusions.

Her trial took place on the morning of November 2. She was accused of seeking to undermine the Republic in her writings, in particular *Les Trois Urnes*. "There can be no doubt," read the prosecution, "of the perfidious intentions and hidden motives of this criminal woman, who in all the works to which she has, at least, lent her name, pours calumny and poison on the warmest defenders of the people." Having been denied the right to counsel, Olympe de Gouges conducted her own defence, playing to the audience with shrugs and expressive gestures, raising her eyes to heaven when the charges were read out. To the accusation of slandering the people's friends (Robespierre and others) she replied with spirit: "My sentiments have not changed and I still hold the same opinion about them. I regard them and always will regard them, as ambitious and self-seeking men." Before her sentence was pronounced, she was asked, as was the custom, if she had anything to say. Her answer sent a ripple of laughter through the court. "My enemies," she declared, "will not have the satisfaction of shedding my blood. I am pregnant and am going to give a citizen or citizenness to the Republic."

Even at the height of the Terror, pregnant women could not be sent to the guillotine. Olympe de Gouges was sentenced to death, subject to a gynaecological examination. Two doctors and a midwife examined her that afternoon but, despite her insistence, could find no certain signs of pregnancy. The fact that she was forty-five – though admitting to only thirty-eight in court – was against her. So too was her three months' imprisonment, though this was not necessarily conclusive. Communications between men and women had been freely possible in the infirmary; even in the Conciergerie the parlour where men and women could circulate in the daytime was known as a Cythera, where snatched encounters in dark corners were an everyday occurrence.

Perhaps Olympe de Gouges's plea was genuine; more likely it was the thought of her son, Pierre Aubry, which had led her to make her final desperate bid for life. Her last letter, written on the evening of her exectuion, was to him. "I die, my son," she wrote, "the victim of my idolatry of my country and of the people. Their enemies, beneath the specious mask of republicanism, have led me remorselessly to the scaffold. . . . Farewell my son, when you receive this letter, I will be no more."

The next morning she listened impassively as her sentence of death was confirmed. On her way to have her hair cut for the execution, a young man tossed a bunch of violets to her. She sniffed them smilingly, and coquettish to the last demanded a mirror to look at her face before being led out to the tumbril.

Ten days after her execution her son, who had been suspended from his duties, signed a "profession of civic faith", denying all sympathy with his mother's views and protesting his own patriotism. With his life in the balance, he could not altogether be blamed; but Olympe de Gouges, with every other ideal shattered, was lucky perhaps to be spared this final disillusion.

Chapter 16

Execrated in life the Queen, Madame Roland and Olympe de Gouges were linked together in death as their common fate was used to give a lesson to their sex. "In the space of a short time," wrote the *Moniteur Universel* of November 19, "the Revolutionary Tribunal has given an example to women which will doubtless not be lost on them; for justice, always impartial, offers instructions along with severity.

"Marie Antoinette, brought up in a treacherous and ambitious court, brought her family's vices to France; she sacrificed her husband, her children and her adopted country to the house of Austria whose aims she served. . . . She was a bad mother, a debauched wife, and she died covered with the curses of those whose ruin she had sought to bring about. Her name will always be regarded with horror by posterity.

"Olympe de Gouges, born with an exalted imagination, took her delirium for an inspiration of nature. She began by losing her mind and ended by adopting the project of the traitors who wished to divide France; she wished to become a public figure, and the law has punished her as a conspirator who ignored the virtues of her sex.

"The Roland woman, petty philosopher and small time intellectual . . . surrounded by mercenary writers to whom she gave suppers and distributed favours, was a monster from every point of view. Her disdainful manner towards the people and the judges chosen by them, her arrogantly self-opinionated answers, her ironic gaiety and the firmness of her bearing on the journey from the Palais de Justice to the Place de la Révolution, prove that no sorrowful feelings occupied her mind. And yet she was a mother;

but she sacrificed nature in her wish to rise above it; her desire to be an intellectual led her to forget the virtues of her sex and this forgetfulness, always dangerous, finally led her to the scaffold."

The lesson was clear: women who interfered in politics, from whatever viewpoint, must expect to reap the consequences of their presumption. It was a message with special reference to women's clubs and organisations, above all the Républicaines-Révolutionnaires. Inevitable casualties in the Jacobin campaign to bring the *sans-culottes* to heel, their downfall and suppression had paralleled the executions of the previous month.

To some extent the Républicaines-Révolutionnaires had played into the government's hands. Not content with harrying the National Convention with their demands for strict control of prices, and stronger measures against "traitors", they had become involved in a series of street battles with the fishwives and market women of Paris, opposed by their profession to the idea of price controls, and far more moderate in their sympathies. A symbolic issue, the wearing of the revolutionary *bonnet rouge*, or red cap, sparked off the discord between the two groups. Having already successfully campaigned to make all women wear a revolutionary cockade, the Républicaines-Révolutionnaires now sought to go one further in imposing the wearing of the *bonnet rouge*. It was intended as a demonstration of patriotism, as a sign of national resistance when the country was in danger. For the fishwives and market women, at a time of acute food shortages, it was the final straw. Already many of them had flung off their cockades as a protest; they responded to the new demands of the Républicaines-Révolutionnaires with the outright violence. A number of their leading members were seized and flogged; the fishwives, reported one newspaper, used the most *striking* arguments to put their point of view. The climax came when the premises of the Républicaines-Révolutionnaires were invaded by a horde of angry women; fighting broke out and the police had to be called in to restore order.

It was the excuse that the government had been looking for. On October 30, in a report presented to the National Convention, it was proposed that all women's clubs should be suppressed and all public assemblies of women forbidden. Taking the disorderly conduct of the Républicaines-Révolutionnaires as his starting point the speaker, the Jacobin deputy André Amar, moved on to general principles. His committee, he announced, had addressed itself to two main questions: were women capable of taking part in government, and should they be allowed to meet in clubs and popular assemblies? To both of these questions he could only answer in the negative. The art of government demanded "extensive knowledge, unlimited attention and devotion, a strict impartiality and self abnegation"; few women possessed such qualities. As for their participation in clubs and popular assemblies their volatile emotions and lack of moral education made them equally unsuited for such activities.

What was the place of women in society? "Morality and nature itself have assigned her functions to her: to begin the education of men, to prepare the minds and hearts of children for the exercise of public virtues, to direct them early in life towards the good, to elevate their souls, to educate them in the cult of liberty – such are their functions after household cares. . . . When they have carried out these duties they will have deserved well of the fatherland."

With only one dissenting voice, the motion suppressing women's clubs was passed; even were no principles involved, said a final speaker, the women's clubs had shown themselves to be dangerous to the Republic, and for that reason alone should be suppressed.

It was not to be expected that the Républicaines-Révolutionnaires would take their dispersal lying down. Denied access to the National Convention, a deputation led by Claire Lacombe and wearing the famous *bonnets rouges* presented itself before the Council of the Paris Commune. But their protests went unheard, giving rise instead to yet another lecture as, amidst furious hooting and cries of "off with the women's red caps", the chairman, Pierre Chaumette denounced them:

"It is horrible, it is contrary to all the laws of nature for a woman to want to make herself a man. . . . Since when is it decent to see women abandoning the pious cares of their households, the cribs of their children, to come to public places to harangue in the galleries? . . . Impudent women, who want to become men, aren't you well enough provided for? What else do you need? Your despotism is the only one our strength cannot resist, since it is the despotism of love, and consequently the work of nature. In the name of this same nature, remain what you are; far from envying us the perils of a stormy life, be content to make us forget them in the heart of our families, in resting our eyes on the enchanting spectacle of our children made happy by your cares."

Such dulcet arguments concealed an underlying ferocity. The examples of Madame Roland and Olympe de Gouges were there to be seen. By mid-November the leading Enragés were in prison or in hiding; threatened with the same fate, Claire Lacombe and Pauline Léon had no choice but to fall silent. In the fraternal societies of Paris, and in clubs in the provinces where women, in many cases, had taken over the functions of the old religious orders in caring for the sick and needy, women continued to play a part for a time. But the grand impetus was over; in the atmosphere of the Terror individual initiatives, however well-intentioned, were too risky to undertake.

Chaumette's anti-feminism reflected not only political expediency but the new-found puritanism of Robespierre's "virtuous republic". Even prostitutes were called to order. The streets were cleared of street walkers; the Palais Egalité, formerly the Palais Royal, haunt of every kind of vice and immorality, was raided by the police. Patrols of citizens were formed to report on "violations of morality"; the sale of "licentious" books and prints was prohibited. Immorality, proclaimed Chaumette, was the last remaining vestige of fourteen centuries of corruption under the monarchy.

At the same time that women, on grounds of morals or expediency, were being forced back into private life, a chosen few were offered a symbolic public role. As goddesses of Reason, in the newly instituted state religion of that name, they presided over festivals all over France. The Jacobin government, while denying women the right of political expression, had no objection to placing them on an official pedestal.

In October 1793 the Revolutionary Calendar had been introduced, substituting the date of September 22, 1792, the first day of the Republic, for the beginning of the Christian era. In a formal policy of de-christianisation the names of the saints' days and religious festivals were replaced by purely secular terms; the year was divided into ten new months; the tenth day, Decadi, took the place of Sunday as a day of rest. Churches were desecrated, the words "Death is an eternal sleep" were printed above the entrances to cemeteries. In early November the Bishop of Paris publicly abjured his faith. Notre Dame was taken over as a Temple of Reason, and a festival to inaugurate the new cult was planned for 20 Brumaire (November 10). The Temple required its tutelary deity, a living figure – since a statue might recall the Virgin Mary – who could be changed from festival to festival. The chosen goddesses, it was decreed, were to be chosen amongst persons "whose character renders beauty respectable and whose severity of morals and manners repulses license". It was an ideal not always realised; festivals of Reason, more often than not, degenerated into saturnalia.

The opening festival took place as planned in Notre Dame. The cathedral had been stripped of its religious ornaments, and a Temple of Philosophy erected in the aisle. The goddess of Reason, a well known actress, Mademoiselle Maillard, dressed in white with a long blue cloak and scarlet cap of liberty, was carried in procession to the Temple and enthroned to the strains of the "Ça ira" and the "Marseillaise". "Chaste ceremony, sad, dry and boring," commented Michelet in his *Femmes de la Révolution*. Years after, in some provincial town, he met a former goddess of Reason, who had taken part in the festivals of 1793, an exemplary matron, chosen for her height and blameless morals. She had never been beautiful, he noted wryly, "and what is more, she squinted."

★ ★ ★

Bordeaux, like Paris, had its festival of Reason. The former stronghold of the Girondins was now in the forefront of Jacobin extremism. On October 10, 1793, four commissioners from Paris had ridden into the town at the head of their troops. Their leader was a man whose cruelty and ruthlessness had already spread fear around the neighbouring countryside. He was the former secretary of the Commune, Jean-Lambert Tallien.

Within days of Tallien's arrival a guillotine had been erected in the main square, a grim counterpoint to the celebrations for the Festival of Reason which accompanied the looting of the churches in the town. "All the prostitutes and criminals of the place had been gathered together," wrote Madame de la Tour du Pin. "They had been decked out in the most beautiful ornaments from the sacristies of the cathedral, of Saint-Seurin and Saint-Michel, churches more ancient than the town itself, endowed with the rarest and most precious objects. These miserable creatures paraded through the quays and principal streets; carts carried what they had not been able to put on themselves. They arrived thus, preceded by the Goddess of Reason, represented by I know not what horrible creature, at the Place de la Comédie, where all those beautiful objects were burned on an enormous bonfire."

The arrival of the Jacobins in Bordeaux had coincided with the birth of Madame de la Tour du Pin's baby. Her husband had stayed to be with her, and the pangs of the birth, she wrote, were as nothing compared to her fears for his safety. Arrests had taken place in many of the neighbouring houses and there was no telling whose turn would be next. An hour after the baby, a daughter, was born, he left Bordeaux to take temporary refuge on his family estate. Neither of them knew what fate lay in store, or when they would meet again. Soon after a warrant was issued for his arrest. Escaping in the nick of time, he went into hiding with a locksmith who for a considerable sum of money arranged to conceal him in a tiny windowless room above his workshop. "I have since visited this miserable hole," wrote Madame de la Tour du Pin. "Only a thin plank floor separated him from the workshop where the apprentices worked and where the forge and bellows were. When the locksmith and his wife left the room next door, always taking the key with them, my husband had to lie stretched on the bed, in order to avoid making the slightest noise. He had been warned that he could have no light, for fear that it would be noticed in the workshop below." Here for the next three months he remained concealed, keeping in contact with his wife through the services of a former groom, who arranged to take messages between them.

Meanwhile Madame de la Tour du Pin, barely recovered from her confinement, had been forced to leave the house outside Bordeaux where she was staying – her host had been placed under house arrest in the town, and it was feared that his country property would be sequestered too. She was offered a refuge in Bordeaux itself, a dilapidated apartment at the back of a big town house belonging to a certain Bonie, who passed in public for a violent Jacobin, but who had been touched by her misfortunes. Here, with her baby and her little boy, attended by her faithful nurse and her negro servant Zamore, she could feel herself safe for the time being.

But there was no escaping the horrors of the world outside. Since Tallien's arrival in Bordeaux the Terror had been in full swing. Not a day passed without its executions. From her apartment near the central square she could hear the rolling of the drums which preceded the fall of each head. The Girondin sympathisers on the city council had been the first to go; their fate was followed by that of numerous leading citizens whose wealth fell victim to the State – or in part to Tallien himself, for he combined corruption with his ruthlessness. It was a time when Fouché in Lyon was gunning down prisoners by the score in order to speed up the rate of executions, when the mass drownings of prisoners in Nantes had poisoned the river with the boatloads of dead bodies. Tallien, less fanatical, was relatively more moderate in his excesses. With his fellow commissioner, Ysabeau, he enjoyed the luxuries and appurtenances that went with power. While Bordeaux fought with famine, with bread queues forming overnight to get their meagre ration of barely edible black bread, the commissioners' servants broke through the ranks of hungry citizens to collect the finest foods and wines for their masters' tables.

Not content with the high style of living to which his role as commissioner had entitled him, Tallien had found a mistress too to fulfil the wildest dreams of every sybarite. In late October, along with scores of others, Thérésia de Fontenay had been arrested on the grounds of lacking proper papers. For one like Tallien, supremely fascinated by money, the daughter of the Spanish banker Cabarrus, with financial contacts across Europe, would always have been a figure of interest. The fact that she was young and beautiful added a new dimension to the situation. The commissioner, coarse, self-seeking, stained with blood, fell madly in love. Thérésia de Fontenay, faced with the choice between prison and life as Tallien's mistress had no hesitation which to choose; Tallien was a "lifeline" in the midst of danger. In early November she moved into the Hôtel Franklin where Tallien had his headquarters in the centre of the town.

★   ★   ★

Almost immediately Thérésia de Fontenay, or Cabarrus as she was now more often known, became the uncrowned queen of Bordeaux. In the midst of misery and terror her salon in the Hôtel Franklin was an oasis of luxury and refinement. One had the impression, wrote a visitor, of entering a sanctuary of the Muses. A piano, with music lying open, rubbed shoulders with an easel on which a painting had just been begun. There was a guitar on the sofa, a harp in the corner, paint brushes, books and an embroidery frame. Tall windows opened on to a balcony with orange trees; at night a table laden with silver would be brought in for supper, Thérésia presiding as Tallien returned from his day's work of arrests and executions.

Nor did she lack her share of public worship. Relaxed and radiantly beautiful, wearing a broad tricolour sash, she would ride with Tallien through the town. On December 30 when Toulon – thanks to a gaunt young artillery officer, Napoleon Bonaparte –

had been recaptured from the British she presided over the celebrations to mark the victory. The scene was the Temple of Reason where, at the climax of the day's processions, she emerged to read a speech extolling liberty. Admirably dressed in a deep blue riding habit, with a fur trimmed red velvet hat on the short dark curls that clustered *à la Titus* round her head, she had never appeared to greater advantage.

The other side of Thérésia's great position to which she rose with real showmanship was soon to be revealed. Almost from the first, sickened by the killings which were going on in Bordeaux, she had used her influence to persuade Tallien towards mercy. Once she had rescued an entire troop of actors and actresses whom her lover had condemned to death; her influence, on countless occasions, was entirely to the good. Tallien was venal; he could be induced to spare his victims if the rewards were big enough. Thérésia, though not averse to receiving gifts from grateful suppliants, acted chiefly from the generosity of her heart. Her task was not always easy: but behind the beauty and abundant vitality of her twenty years she hid a shrewd and active brain. She knew how to use her charms to bring Tallien, and sometimes his colleagues, round, when to act openly, and when to work by subterfuge. The proof of her influence was dramatically displayed. In the months from December 1793 to March 1794 the number of executions dropped by almost half from the average of the previous two months. Years later, when, thanks to her easy reputation and association with Tallien, she found herself ostracised from society, she would sometimes be snubbed, as she bitterly remarked, by some of those very aristocrats whose lives she had saved.

There was one person by whom she would always be remembered with gratitude. Madame de la Tour du Pin had known Thérésia, then little more than a child, in Paris, in the first years of her marriage to the Marquis de Fontenay. With infinite trepidation, for the danger of discovery might outweigh any chance of help, she wrote to ask her for a moment's interview. The warmth of Thérésia's welcome was all that she could wish, and Madame de la Tour du Pin's description, perhaps better than any other, gives an impression of the beauty that had taken Tallien by storm. "Her features," she wrote, "were perfect in their regularity. Her hair, ebony black, was like the finest silk, and nothing could dim the radiance of her wonderfully clear complexion. An enchanting smile revealed a glimpse of perfect teeth. Her height recalled that of Diana the Huntress. Her slightest movement had a matchless grace. Her melodious voice, with its trace of a foreign accent, had a charm impossible to convey. It was painful to think that so much youth, beauty, grace and wit were abandoned to a man who every morning consigned so many innocent people to their death."

Through Thérésia Cabarrus, Madame de la Tour du Pin was put in touch with Tallien whose protection was her best hope of survival. She approached his presence almost fainting with horror; had he been her executioner, he wrote, she could have felt no more. The monster of her anticipation proved to be a good-looking young man of twenty-five or six, with a mop of curly blonde hair and an expression he strove hard to make severe.

"Is it you then," he demanded, "who is the daughter-in-law of that man who was confronted with the widow Capet?" (At the trial of the Queen the former minister had refused to refer to her as "the Woman Capet", continuing to speak of her as "Her Majesty" in defiance of the Prosecutor's orders.) "And you have a father? . . . What is his name? Ah, Dillon. The General? . . . All these enemies of Republic will have to go," and he made a beheading gesture with his hand.

Madame de la Tour du Pin forgot her fear in indignation. "I have not come here, Citizen," she said, "to hear the death warrant of my relatives, and since you cannot help me, I shall importune you no further."

She returned home convinced that she had made her situation even worse than before. But Thérésia reassured her; she had made a favourable impression on Tallien, she told her, and he had promised that she would not be arrested.

Despite this, her situation was becoming more dangerous each day. Tallien's influence was not all powerful; his colleague, Ysabeau, more ferocious than he, was already complaining of his moderation. Her husband was once more on the run; the locksmith, terrified for his life, had refused to hide him any more. She dared not bring him to Bordeaux for fear that the nursemaid, whose loyalty she suspected, would denounce him. She was almost at her wits' end, unable to sleep, terrified by every knock on the door, when a notice in the local paper, glimpsed idly one morning, gave her a sudden cry of hope. It announced the departure of an American ship, the *Diana*, in eight days' time; it was the first to be allowed to leave Bordeaux, where more than eighty American ships had been languishing in harbour for more than a year. In an instant her mind was made up; they would leave for America the following week.

With the help of a shipping agent, an old friend of her father's, she was able to obtain places for herself, her husband and her two children on the *Diana*. An order from Tallien, authorising the issue of four passports under assumed names, gave her the confidence to send a message to her husband. Her host, Bonie, undertook to escort him on the perilous journey to Bordeaux; armed with false papers and disguised in peasant's clothes he made his way down river by night, and was hidden by Bonie in an upstairs room.

Two days before the ship was due to sail, they presented themselves with their passport applications at the Hôtel de Ville. They had waited till evening in the hope that they would not be recognised in the poor light. Madame de la Tour du Pin, carrying her baby and holding her little boy by the hand, kept well apart from her husband, in the darkest corner of the room. When, at the moment of registering the passport, the Town Clerk, wearing his red cap, asked her husband to remove his hat so that he could record his description, the little boy covered his face with his hands and flung himself against his mother. He was only four, but he sensed the danger to his father.

Even now, with the passports issued, it remained to get them signed. Trusting in Tallien's good will, Madame de la Tour du Pin hastened to see Thérésia Cabarrus. She found her in tears; two hours earlier Tallien had been recalled to Paris; it was Ysabeau who was to sign the passports. Providence, in the guise of Tallien's former secretary, who had remained behind to work for Ysabeau, came to their aid. His new master, he explained would be signing papers at ten that evening, after coming from the theatre; as he was always in a hurry for his supper he would scarcely look at what he was signing. This proved to be the case; as the secretary entered Thérésia's salon with the passports in his hand, both she and Madame de la Tour du Pin fell on his neck and embraced him.

On March 10, on the pretext of taking the children for a walk, Madame de la Tour du Pin left the house where she had spent five anxious months, and made her way to the *Diana*. Her baggage was already on board; her husband, who had been in hiding at the house of the Dutch consul, rejoined her on the boat that was to take them downstream to the ship. The captain took the rudder, with a cry of "Off!" the boat was cast loose from the shore. "A feeling of indescribable happiness came over me," wrote Madame de la Tour du Pin. "Seated opposite my husband, whose life I was saving, with my two children on my knee, everything seemed possible. Poverty, work, misery, nothing was difficult with him beside me. Ah! Without question that thrust of the oars which the sailor gave to launch us from the shore, marked the happiest moment of my existence."

Chapter 17

Tallien returned to Paris in March 1794 in a state of understandable apprehension. Denounced by his colleagues for moderation, it was in reality his corruption while in office at Bordeaux that was chiefly held against him. If Thérésia, for the most part, had been activated by good-heartedness, Tallien had lost no opportunity to profit from his leniency; to the loot acquired by pillage was added the ransoms of those he had saved. His blatant affair with Thérésia, the former marquise, was a further liability – his first infatuation over, he began to realise the dangers she brought with her. Despite her desire to follow him, he had no intention of bringing her to Paris.

If the atmosphere in the capital had been sinister that autumn, it was now still further charged with terror. The Revolution, like Saturn, was devouring its own children. Robespierre, a virtual dictator, presided over Paris with an iron hand. On March 24 Hébert, the scurrilous editor of the *Père Duchesne*, the self-appointed spokesman of the *sans-culottes*, went to "sneeze into the basket", as he had so often rejoiced at seeing others do. He had represented the violent and extremist Left, closely connected with the Enragés. But those who preached moderation were equally at risk. In December 1793 Camille Desmoulins had published the famous first number of his paper *Le Vieux Cordelier*, proposing a "committee of clemency". The young man who, in his own eyes, had launched the Revolution was now calling for it to stop. In the following issue, recalling the atmosphere of Rome under Nero, he drew an analogy with the Paris of the day. Called to order by Robespierre, he refused to cease printing; when he was threatened that his offices would be closed down and copies of his paper burned, he replied in the words of Rousseau: "Burning is not an answer." His young wife, Lucile, supported him. "Let him be," she said to those who begged him to desist, "let him fulfil his mission. . . . And anyone who disagrees with me shall not have any of my chocolate."

Such acts of defiance, inspired by genuine idealism, carried the seeds of their destruction with them. In early April, together with Danton and fourteen others, the "Indulgents" as they were called, Desmoulins was arrested. Involved in financial scandals, Danton had an element of self-interest in his bid for clemency which he hoped would win support in the Convention, and divert attention from his peccadilloes. But he was sickened too by the bloodshed of the time, and he reached heroic stature at his trial and death.

The trial of Danton, Desmoulins and their companions, as much a travesty as that of the Girondins had been, brought its inevitable verdict. Desmoulins had wept with remorse when the Girondins were condemned – his scathing pen, in a pamphlet, *L'Histoire des Brissotins*, had done more than any other to stir up hatred against them. Now about to share their fate, he could feel himself to some extent redeemed by his courageous stand. "I am thirty-three," he declared proudly in court, "the same age as the *sans-culotte* Jesus." But despair overcame him when writing to his wife. His farewell letter remains one of the most moving documents of the Revolution. "Goodbye, Loulou," he concluded, "goodbye, my life, my soul, my divinity on earth . . . I feel the shores of life receding from me. I still see Lucile! I see her! My crossed arms embrace you, my bound hands clasp you, my severed head reposes on your breast."

The next day, April 5, he went with Danton to the guillotine, his courage failing him completely; weeping and cursing, he struggled to free himself from his bonds. His final words were of Lucile: "My wife, my beloved, I shall never see you again." Danton, undaunted to the end, was the last of the batch to be executed. "Show my head to the people," he told the executioner. "It is worth seeing."

Lucile Desmoulins followed her husband to the scaffold only five days later. Arrested on a trumped-up charge, she had little interest in continuing to live. Her son, Horace, was entrusted to her mother, and it was to her she wrote her final note: "Good night, mama. A tear falls from my eyes. It is for you. I fall asleep in the calm of innocence." The note, like so many other last messages, was never delivered. It was found, years later, in the files of the public prosecutor.

In a Paris palpitating with dramatic events, Tallien knew he must tread with the utmost caution. Within days of his arrival he was gathering his supporters in the National Convention. Irresistibly talkative – Robespierre described him as a "tap of tepid water" – he spouted fine and patriotic phrases, he inveighed against the enemies of the Republic in furious speeches from the tribune, and was soon so successfully established that he was elected President of the Convention.

In Bordeaux, Thérésia Cabarrus's situation was becoming increasingly uneasy. Deprived of her lover's support, she found herself shunned by the other members of the commission there. From Paris, Tallien, in an attempt to show her in a suitably patriotic light, had sent her the text of a petition to the National Convention. She signed it and returned it as her own. Not for her the claims for women's rights which had led Olympe de Gouges to the scaffold. Specifically disclaiming all thoughts of equality between the sexes – "women should be companions, not rivals to men" – it called for a return to the domestic virtues. "Now more than ever," it declared, "morality is the order of the day"; it was the role of women to give an example by their conduct, and when not occupied with their duties as wives and mothers, to devote themselves to the care of the sick and the unfortunate.

These high flown sentiments made little impression on the National Convention. Thérésia's motives were too obvious, her immorality too well known, to carry conviction. Meanwhile Condorcet, in hiding since the downfall of the Girondins, was completing his last great work, *Esquisse d'un tableau historique des progrès de l'esprit humain*, maintaining to the last his championship of women: "The complete destruction of the legal inequality between men and women, fatal even to those it favours, is one of the essential conditions of human progress." His time was running out. On April 5, fearing that his continued presence might endanger his hostess, he left his hiding place and went out into the countryside. He was arrested two days later, and found dead, most probably from poison, in his cell the following morning.

Thérésia Cabarrus had no such heroism in her make-up. Her petition to the Convention had done nothing to improve her position. A new commissioner from Paris had arrived in Bordeaux to seek for evidence of Tallien's corruption – the evidence would not be hard to find. Availing herself of a new law which forebade former members of the aristocracy to reside in frontier or coastal towns, she obtained a passport to leave Bordeaux. She entrusted her two year old son to a servant there, and set out first to Orléans and then to Paris. She did not go unaccompanied. A new admirer, a certain Jean Guéry, was her companion on her journey. Her movements had been followed by Robespierre's spies – his eyes were firmly on Tallien, and he hoped to entrap him through his former mistress. But the spies found no evidence of political intrigue; her correspondence, one of them reported, contained nothing suspect, the subjects were all "*en amoroso*".

Thérésia knew that she was being watched. She knew too that she could not rely on Tallien. Despite his success in being voted President of the National Convention, he had been violently attacked by Robespierre in a recent session. The Convention, part terrorised, part mesmerised by Robespierre, was still under his spell; those he attacked felt dangerously close to the scaffold.

Robespierre, perhaps, was not yet strong enough to strike at Tallien directly, but he had no compunction about lesser fry. On May 22, after weeks of desperate tacking from hiding place to hiding place, Thérésia and her presumed lover, Guéry, were arrested. Tallien, under threat himself, could do nothing openly to help her. Refusing a request from his local revolutionary committee to intervene on behalf of Guéry, he went on to repudiate Thérésia too. "As for the woman arrested with him," he wrote, "I knew her in Bordeaux where I was sent as a Representative of the People, but it is four months [sic] since I returned to Paris. I do not know what has taken place since that time, and I do not wish to interfere in any way. The authorities who have arrested these people have their reasons. They will hasten to render them the justice they deserve. A representative of the people would betray his duty and vilify his character if he intervened on behalf of suspected persons." In fact, he had been in touch with her several times during the weeks before her arrest. Both knew too much to betray one another. Despite repeated questioning Thérésia said nothing to compromise her former lover. She knew that her safety, and her chance of surviving, depended on his.

★ ★ ★

Two months earlier, on March 19, Joséphine de Beauharnais had been arrested. She, too, had found Tallien a man of straw when she turned to him for help. Her son Eugène, recalled her daughter Hortense in her memoirs, had rushed off to see Tallien and tell him of their misfortune. "Alas! he who woud have been willing to help us was powerless to do so. Terror had frozen every heart."

Joséphine was taken to the prison of Les Carmes; her husband Alexandre had been arrested just before her, and the couple, separated for more than six years, were now united under the same roof. In January, hearing that he was threatened, she had written to the Committee of Public Security, ostensibly on behalf of her sister-in-law who had recently been arrested and whose husband, Alexandre's elder brother, was an émigré. "I should be very sorry, Citizen Representative," she wrote, "if you should confuse Alexandre with the elder Beauharnais. . . . You may doubt the patriotism of the former nobility but it is always possible that there may be ardent friends of Liberty and Equality among them. Alexandre has never deviated from these principles; he has always marched in step. If he were not a republican he would not have my esteem and friendship. I am an American, and know only him of his family. My household is a republican household. Before the Revolution my children were not distinguishable from *sans-culottes* and I hope they will be worthy of the Republic. I write to you frankly as a *sans-culotte* . . . I appeal to your sympathy and

141

humanity on behalf of an unfortunate citizeness."

The letter, though of no avail to save her husband or her sister-in-law, had probably helped to draw attention to her. Had she stayed quietly in Croissy, avoiding notice, she might have managed to escape arrest.

Courageous though her plea had been, Joséphine showed little sign of courage once she reached the prison of Les Carmes. She wept almost continuously, recalled her cellmate Delphine de Custine, embarrassing her companions by her lack of spirit. There was indeed enough to make her weep. The prison of Les Carmes was described with small exaggeration as an Augean stable. Overcrowded, the air foul from the smell of the latrine buckets set along the corridors, it lacked even the amenities that Madame Roland had been offered; the prison food was filthy, the inmates were crowded as many as fourteen to a cell.

In the garden of the prison where the sexes were allowed to mingle at certain times of the day, Joséphine de Beauharnais once more met her husband. Priggish to the end, he had little natural sympathy with the wife he had always disapproved of as frivolous and light-minded. In the hectic atmosphere of prison life, where every day might be the last, he had fallen in love with Delphine de Custine; Joséphine in her turn, or so her detractors had it afterwards, was enjoying a brief affair with a dashing young general, Lazare Hoche. But husband and wife were united in their love for their children. Eugène and Hortense, now aged thirteen and eleven, strove pathetically to get letters through to their parents and, when letters were forbidden, wrote out the laundry lists sent in each week in a mute effort to communicate. Once, wrote Hortense, they were able to catch a glimpse of their parents from a window of the prison, but the window was blocked up and they were never to see their father again.

On July 22 Alexandre de Beauharnais was taken to the Conciergerie; he was tried and executed two days later. In his farewell letter to Joséphine, which was later published as a pamphlet, he begged her to clear his memory and to recall his services to the Republic. "Goodbye," he concluded, "you know those I love; be their comforter and by your care prolong my life in their hearts. Goodbye, I press you and my dear children to my heart for the last time." To Delphine de Custine he left a ring; she would treasure it for the rest of her life.

When the news of his death reached Joséphine, she collapsed completely. It was a collapse which probably saved her life. Her own trial was to have followed her husband's immediately but she was judged to be too weak to move and remained prostrated in her cell.

Chapter 18

In the prison of La Force, Thérésia Cabarrus was enduring conditions as loathsome as those that Joséphine was undergoing. She would recall with horror the straw mattress crawling with vermin which was her bed, the fetid water and black bread which was her diet. Later she would take pleasure in dramatising her sufferings; as the acknowledged Queen of the Directoire she would display her sandalled feet with rings on her toes which concealed, she declared, the scars left by rats which had bitten them in prison. But for the time being, like Joséphine, she was apathetic with misery, ignorant, like all her fellow prisoners, of the dramas which were taking place outside.

On June 10, two weeks after her arrest, the infamous law of 22 Prairial was passed, refusing suspects the right of counsel and allowing only one of two verdicts – acquittal or death. The terror was reaching a crescendo. The guillotine had had to be removed from the Place de la Révolution; the stench of blood had become too great for the inhabitants to endure and it had been transported to an open space on the outskirts of the city. The number of executions now averaged sixty a day but the crowds that used to flock to them were jaded; only a hardened core of *tricoteuses* remained as regular spectators.

The "Republic of Virtue" which was Robespierre's dream was being imposed by terror; at the same time it was being celebrated in a new religion. Robespierre had never approved of the cult of Reason, nor the atheism it proclaimed. On June 8 he inaugurated the Festival of the Supreme Being, confirming the Revolution's belief in God and the immortal soul. Clad in a sky blue coat and yellow breeches, his hair carefully powdered, a bunch of flowers in his hand, he led the Convention in a procession through the streets of Paris to the Champ de Mars. In front of an immense crowd, carrying flowers and garlands, he ceremoniously set fire to the effigies of Atheism, Ambition and Egoism; the statue of Wisdom, her face much blackened by soot, rose phoenix-like from the flames.

"Today," declared Robespierre, in his address to the crowd, "let us give ourselves up to transports of joy; tomorrow we shall return to the fight against tyranny and crime." The warning was clear; there was to be no abatement in the Terror.

Having disposed of the "moderates" in the form of Danton and Desmoulins, and the extremists in the form of Hébert, it was corruption that Robespierre now sought to eliminate from his ideal republic. A clause in the law of 22 Prairial had suspended the immunity of members of the National Convention from prosecution; those who, like Tallien, had used their missions in the provinces to enrich themselves, felt particularly under threat. But they were not alone in the atmosphere of terror and suspicion that pervaded the Convention. During the month of June, it is recorded, more than sixty members of the Convention slept away from their homes each night, fearful of the knock on the door which heralded arrest.

Terrified for his own life, and working on the fears of others, Tallien, with Fouché, responsible for countless deaths in Lyon, and Barras, equally bloodstained from missions in Toulon and Marseille, spent the first weeks of July in weaving the conspiracy that would lead to Robespierre's overthrow. They knew their time was short. In the National Convention, Couthon, Robespierre's ally, spoke openly of them as rascals, "whose hands are full of the wealth of the Republic". On July 14 Fouché was expelled from the Jacobin Club; three days later Tallien suffered the same fate.

On the side of the conspirators was the growing public revulsion against the Terror; French victories in recent months had removed the threat of invasion which had been its chief justification. With skill and subtlety, Fouché went from deputy to deputy planting the seeds of fear. Whom would Robespierre strike next? As long as he lived no one was safe. On July 26, unknowingly playing into Fouché's hands, Robespierre made a two hour speech in the National Convention, painting a picture of a conspiracy among the members, but postponing the announcement of the names of those involved.

It was the moment the conspirators had been waiting for, the moment too, according to Thérésia's version of events, when Tallien's flagging courage was spurred by a message from his mistress in La Force.

"The administrator of the police had just left," she wrote; "he came to tell me that tomorrow I go to the tribunal, that is to say, the scaffold. How different this seems from a dream I had last night; Robespierre no longer existed, and the prisons were open. But thanks to your notable cowardice there will soon be no one left in France to realise it." With this letter, according to this same account, was a Spanish dagger with which he was to arm himself.

The story, though romantic, was certainly untrue. Thérésia had been stripped and searched (in front of eight men) on her entrance into prison. She had no chance of keeping a dagger in her possession. Nor was it likely, given the danger of her letter being intercepted, that she would have dared send such a message to her lover – a certain death sentence for both if it were discovered. But the legend of her intervention would weave itself round the events of July 27 – 9 Thermidor – heightening, if it were possible, the drama of the day.

The morning of 9 Thermidor saw the National Convention crowded to its limits. Robespierre's expected statement on the conspiracy, and a sense that something momentous was pending, had filled the galleries to overflowing. It was Saint-Just, Robespierre's icy *alter ego*, who made the opening speech. Before he could get into his stride he was violently interrupted by Tallien: "Yesterday a member of the government [Robespierre] isolated himself, delivering a speech in his own name; today another is doing the same thing. They are trying to precipitate the country into an abyss. I ask that the veil be entirely torn aside."

It was the start of the furious exchanges, heard first with horror, then with growing approval, by the Convention, which would lead to the arrest of Robespierre. It was Tallien, once again, who came to the fore when Robespierre tried to speak; such was his ascendancy over the Convention that he might even have swung them back behind them. Tallien was well aware of this danger, and knew also that he had gone too far to draw back. Amidst shouts of "Down with the tyrant", he rushed to the rostrum before him. Pulling a dagger – the dagger Thérésia claimed was hers – from his coat he brandished it in front of the Convention. "Yesterday," he declared, "I saw the army of the new Cromwell forming and I armed myself with a dagger to pierce his breast if the Convention had not the courage to accuse him."

Shouted down by the Convention, Robespierre was unable to make himself heard. Amidst scenes of indescribable confusion he was arrested at the demand of an obscure Dantonist deputy, together with Saint-Just and three others. Even now his defeat was far from certain. The Commune, having declared itself in a state of insurrection, was rallying the *sans-culottes*; towards evening the arrested deputies were released and made their way to the Hôtel de Ville. But at the moment of crisis Robespierre lacked the decisiveness to take command. The mob, whose power he had helped to break, was without effective leaders; left to themselves they gradually dispersed. Meanwhile Barras had gathered a small army to defend the Convention. At one in the morning, encountering almost no resistance, his troops entered the Hôtel de Ville; Robespierre, his jaw broken by a pistol shot, was taken back to the Convention. That evening, dressed in the same sky blue coat he had worn for the Festival of the Supreme Being, he went to the scaffold. The Terror was over.

★ ★ ★

News of Robespierre's death spread quickly through the Paris prisons where more than eight hundred people were awaiting trial. Years after, when she was Empress, Joséphine de Beauharnais described how it first reached the prison of Les Carmes. Outside the window a woman in the street was attracting attention by her extraordinary antics, repeatedly pointing at her dress to make the first syllable – "*robe*" – of Robespierre's name, then picking up a stone to make the second, "pierre"; finally, with an expressive gesture, she ran her finger across her throat. The dumbshow was interpreted with growing hope. That evening, as if in further confirmation, a warder tripping over a dog in the passage called it Robespierre as he cursed it roundly.

A surge of rejoicing ran through the prisons, through Paris and the whole of France. "Every heart was filled with a feeling of inexpressible joy," wrote Madame de Staël in her history of the Revolution; "human life is such that the end of suffering is the greatest happiness of all." But she had no illusions, either then or later, about the quality of the men who had replaced Robespierre. "The new revolution which has just taken place," she wrote to her husband shortly after 9 Thermidor, "has put villains motivated by self-interest in place of a villain motivated by pure love of crime."

In the prison of La Force, Thérésia Cabarrus might well have expected her instant release. But Tallien, in the wake of Robespierre's downfall, had more important things to think about. The 10 and 11 Thermidor were spent in covering his tracks, in destroying the records of his embezzlements in Bordeaux and establishing his position with the new government. It was public opinion which forced him to turn his attention to Thérésia. Almost immediately, as if from a spontaneous need to shape events, the story that it was love that had driven him to challenge Robespierre had captured the imagination of the public. It was Thérésia's dagger he had brandished, her imminent execution that had spurred him on. The story was too good to deny, especially given his far from spotless record as a terrorist. On the 12 Thermidor, the day of Thérésia's twenty-first birthday, he arrived at the prison to claim her.

A crowd was waiting as she came out. She emerged as a heroine, our Lady of Thermidor, the good angel whose influence had brought the Terror to an end. It did not matter that she did not love, had never loved, Tallien, or that he, intent on his own safety, had given little thought to her. In the eyes of the public they were linked as lovers, and he from self-interest, she from her natural desire to shine, played up to the part. Her two months in prison had done nothing to dim her astonishing beauty. When she rode with Tallien in an open carriage, or appeared in a box at the theatre, they were greeted with acclamation. For the moment she was the most fêted women in Paris and she recognised her almost royal role. "Though I have never been a queen," she recalled in later life, "I have lived for a time in a whirlwind not far different from that which surrounds a throne."

Tallien made the most of his legend, which his colleagues were equally eager to promote. The terrorists who had overthrown Robespierre to save their own skins now found themselves caught up in the overwhelming reaction against the Terror. Some, like Fouché, found it wisest to retire from public life before their crimes could be held against them; others, like Tallien, interpreted the public mood and acted on it. On August 18, in the National Convention, he denounced the Terror as "an instrument of tyranny", and went on to condemn the law which treated noblemen as public enemies. "I no longer recognise castes in the Republic; I see only good citizens and bad. What does it matter to me if a man was born noble if his conduct is good? What difference does the rank of a plebeian make if he is a scoundrel. . . . In France there are only republicans – or anti-republicans who are rogues."

Tallien was tacking to the prevailing wind; over the next few months he established himself as one of the leading members of the new government. The law of 22 Prairial was repealed, the prisons emptied. In November the Jacobins Club was invaded by bands of young men, who threw out its members and manhandled and even flogged the spectators in the galleries. A few days later, the club was closed on the pretext of keeping public order. Thérésia was among the group of deputies who went officially to take the keys; it was her influence, she later claimed, that had helped to bring about the club's demise.

The next month, crowning the legend of her love for Tallien – and perhaps because she was pregnant – Thérésia married Tallien in a civil ceremony. The child of their marriage was christened Rose-Thermidor.

Chapter 19

Joséphine de Beauharnais had been freed from prison soon after Thérésia Cabarrus. It was Thérésia who brought the good news to her children, and Tallien who had been the instrument of her release. "He showed great presence of mind," wrote Hortense in her memoirs, "and when later he asked Mother as a favour to receive the lady he had just married, how could she refuse his request?"

Through her association with Tallien, still tarnished by his record in the Terror, Thérésia had lost face with the survivors of the old régime. Joséphine, the former Vicomtesse de Beauharnais, widow of a general who had fought for the republic, spanned both the old world and the new. In the confused political situation after 9 Thermidor, when the new government strove to follow the tricky path between royalist reaction on the one hand and Jacobin extremism on the other, her social credentials were ideal. Thérésia was the darling of the populace; Joséphine had the charm and elegance of manner to smooth her path in the salons of the new society in Paris, where the remnants of the old aristocracy mixed with the newly rich – the speculators and profiteers who had made money out of the war.

"Nothing could be stranger than the social life in Paris at this time," wrote Madame de Staël. "The influence of women, the ascendancy of good society, what were popularly known as the *gilded salons*, seemed immensely formidable to those who were not admitted and seduced those who were. . . . The converted members of the Jacobin party made their entrance into high society for the first time, and their *amour propre* on everything that pertained to elegant manners was greater than on any other subject. The women of the *ancien régime* surrounded them to obtain the return of their brothers, their sons, their husbands, and the graceful flattery which they knew so well how to use made its mark on those uncouth ears, and disposed the most intransigent politicians towards what we have since seen: that is to say, the re-creation of a court, with all its abuses, but making sure that they were part of it themselves."

The court of which she spoke was, of course, Napoleon's; in the aftermath of Thermidor, however, he was no more than an officer on half pay who had narrowly escaped reprisals for his too-close association with Robespierre. Penniless and unemployed, he looked at the glittering world of post-Thermidorian Paris and described it in a letter to his brother:

"Luxury, pleasure and the arts are picking up in an astonishing manner. Yesterday they gave *Phèdre* at the Opéra for the benefit of a former actress; there were huge crowds from two o'clock onwards although the prices had been trebled. Carriages and elegant folk reappear, forgetting, as though it had been no more than a long dream, that they had ever ceased to shine. Women are everywhere, in the theatres, the promenades, the bookshops. Even in the offices of professors you meet some very pretty creatures. Here, alone, of all places, they deserve to rule; all the men are mad about them, think of nothing but them, and live only for them. A woman needs to live in Paris for six months to know what is due to her, and what her empire is."

In this new world Joséphine and Madame Tallien shone as the brightest stars. Though badly off at first, Joséphine had contrived, through Tallien's help, to reclaim some of her husband's sequestered property. Before long she had become the mistress of Barras who, with Tallien, was one of the leading figures in the new government. But politics had never been an important preoccupation with Joséphine, though money and the security it could bring had inevitably become so. Her family in the West Indies had been ruined by the Revolution; her widowed mother could do little to help her; she was deeply in debt. Barras, corrupt and immensely rich, was as much a "lifeline" for her as Tallien had been for

Thérésia.

Colleagues, rather than rivals in beauty, Thérésia and Joséphine were leaders of fashion in a society that was doing everything to throw off the memories of the last five years and plunge themselves into gaiety and pleasure. Paris danced. Most of the great private houses were now empty, their contents looted, their owners fled. But the theatres were thriving, after the gloomy censorship of the "virtuous republic", dance halls had sprung up all over the city, providing public entertainment for all but the poorest members of society. The most exclusive balls were the "*bals des victimes*", when only relations of those who had perished in the Terror were admitted, and the women wore thin red ribbons round their necks, with their hair cut short, in imitation of those whose locks were shorn for execution. But there were balls at every level, and the new leaders of society, still afraid to show too much ostentation in their entertaining, were happy to take part in them.

There was no lack of ostentation, though, in the fashions of the day. The young men, the "*muscadins*"* or "*incroyables*",† affected absurdly high collars, pinched waists and squared-off coat tails; the most elegant dropped their 'r's in conversation, the word "*parole*" became "*paole*", "*incroyable*" itself was "*incoyable*". Bands of well-off young men, the *jeunesse dorée*, elegantly dressed, with heavy sticks in their hands, roamed Paris to avenge themselves on the Jacobins who had so long held sway; it was the *jeunesse dorée* who had broken into the Jacobins Club in the disturbances that led to its demise.

The costumes of the *jeunesse dorée* looked constricting, with their tight waists and high collars. Those of the women were the opposite. Never had dresses been more scanty or diaphanous, with high waists and low-cut bosoms, their semi-transparent materials leaving little to the imagination. We read of Madame Tallien in floating Grecian draperies, with jewels round her arms and ankles, and skirts slit to the thigh, or Joséphine de Beauharnais, dispensing with a petticoat so as to reveal flesh-coloured satin pantaloons

*Fops or dandies.
†Literally unbelievables.

beneath the flimsiest of muslin dresses. Sometimes the two of them acted in concert. In a letter to Thérésia, Joséphine writes of her plans for a forthcoming ball:

"As it seems important to me that we should be dressed in exactly the same way, I give you notice that I shall have on my hair a red kerchief knotted Creole style with three curls on either side of my brow. What may be rather daring for me will be perfectly normal for you, as you are younger, perhaps no prettier, but infinitely fresher. You see I am fair to everyone. . . . You will understand the importance of this conspiracy, the need for secrecy, and the enormous effect that will result. Till tomorrow, I count on you."

It could hardly be expected that Madame de Staël would remain aloof from this new society and, though her interests were political rather than sartorial, she brought her own fashion note to the scene. It was about this period that she adopted her famous headdress of a turban, and the series of gaudy, semi-oriental stoles with which she draped her fine arms and shoulders.

In March 1795, the first country to do so, Sweden recognised the new French government. The Baron de Staël took up his place in the embassy again. His wife was eager to join him, though a somewhat acrimonious correspondence makes it clear that he was less willing to receive her. He managed to fend her off for two months, even going so far as to send messengers to turn her back on her journey from Switzerland, but it was to no avail. On May 10, accompanied by a new lover, Benjamin Constant, she arrived in Paris to join him. The Baron de Staël announced the news of her arrival "in a stifled voice", and took to his bed for several days before he could face her.

Madame de Staël reopened her salon in the Swedish embassy. Not for her the frivolities of Mesdames Tallien and de Beauharnais. In Switzerland, after Robespierre's fall, she had written a major political pamphlet, *Réflexions sur la Paix addressées à M. Pitt et aux Français*. Its burden was a call for peace. The Jacobin dictatorship was over; France was a republic which would not yield to foreign menaces or the army of the émigrés; it should nonetheless be possible for moderates of all nations to bring to the end a war which benefited no one. (Two extracts from her pamphlet were used by Fox, Pitt's great adversary in Parliament, in his speech against the war that May.)

In Paris she printed a further pamphlet, *Réflexions sur la Paix Intérieure*, in which she welcomed the idea of a republic as the best guarantee of political liberty for France. A monarchy, she wrote, offered too many dangers at the present time, and in a sentence which was to prove prophetic she continued: "France can remain where she is as a republic; but to arrive at a constitutional monarchy she must first pass through a military dictatorship."

Despite her professions of republicanism, she was not a popular figure with the government in France. Her ceaseless efforts for her friends in exile – constitutionalists who had been listed as émigrés and hence risked death if they returned – were too blatant not to irritate the authorities. Though her salon attracted all sections of the new ruling class, it was obvious that her sympathies were with the most moderate elements, those who, though not royalist in sympathy, best represented the aims of 1789. In August 1795 she was denounced in the National Convention as a tool of the émigrés, who used her salon to corrupt unwary deputies, and in the uproar against her that followed judged it wiser to retire from Paris for a while.

★   ★   ★

While luxury and pleasure flourished amongst the richer sections of society, conditions for the poor in Paris had grown steadily worse. With the fall of Robespierre the law of the Maximum, fixing prices for food and basic necessities, was lifted. Prices soared, while the value of *assignats* – the state currency issued at the time of the sale of Church lands – fell disastrously. The winter of 1794–5 was exceptionally severe. Popular discontent reached its climax in the spring. On April 11, 1795 (12 Germinal), there was a mass uprising in the city; the mob invaded the National Convention with a call for bread and the shelved Constitution of 1793.

As on previous *journées* where matters of subsistence were in question – the October days, the riots of 1793 – women were in the forefront of the protestors. But the Jacobins, who had used them to push the Revolution further left, were a spent force; the popular clubs and the Commune had been abolished. Lacking organised support, the mob was easily dispersed, while the women who had taken part were dismissed as furies or viragoes, their lack of femininity deplored by those in power.

Two months later another, a far more serious uprising took place on May 20 (1 Prairial); an armed mob converged on the Convention, demanding the re-establishment of the Commune; in the conflict that followed a deputy was murdered and his head presented on a pike to the president of the assembly. With great difficulty the mob was ejected, and the government used troops to follow up their success, and to crush the *sans-culottes* once and for all.

It was the end of radical protest in Paris, and the end, too, of women's participation in the great mass moments which had helped to shape the Revolution's course. A few days later the Convention passed a decree forbidding women to attend its meetings, unless they were accompanied by a man carrying a citizen's card. At the same time they were ordered off the streets; groups of more than five women were liable to be dispersed by force and held under arrest. It was no wonder that working women, in the police records of the day, were reported as trampling the revolutionary cockade under foot, remarking that it had not been worth while to guillotine the King; a group of others, similarly reported, summed up their plight succinctly: "Eight months ago we had bread and today we don't have it any more. . . . If you go to present a petition about it to the National Convention you are arrested. The popular societies have been closed. We've been plunged back into slavery."

Henceforth, women would remain silent in the political up- heavals which led to the accession of Napoleon. Only Madame de Staël, indefatigably writing and intriguing, passionate, as one biographer put it, in the cause of moderation, continued to try to influence affairs. Her reward would be long years of exile when Napoleon came to power. She had never taken an interest in the fate of her own sex – regarding herself as a being above and almost apart from it. She made no comments on the gradual erosion of women's position which followed the Revolution. Under the Code Napoléon, the laws of divorce would be modified in favour of men. Equality of opportunity in education, which Condorcet at least had preached as an ideal, was no longer a goal. In matters of property women were treated as legal minors, forbidden to make contracts without their husbands' or fathers' consent. Only the laws of inheritance, by which, in 1791, women were legally entitled to an equal share with men, remained unchanged, the one tangible legacy of the Revolution.

Intangibly, though, there had been gains. Women, if only briefly, had felt their power to change events. Feminist heroines like Théroigne de Méricourt and Olympe de Gouges, though ridiculed, were not entirely forgotten; in an age of great men, women like Madame Roland and Charlotte Corday had shown themselves capable of rising to a heroic, if tragic, destiny. Two hundred years later, with a vision far different from theirs, we see them as prophetic figures. But, returning to the Paris of the eighteenth century, it is Joséphine de Beauharnais, not they, who will usher in the Napoleonic age.

★ ★ ★

October 1795 saw a new uprising in Paris, not of the Left but the Right. Since the summer, when an émigré force had landed at Quiberon Bay, only to be crushed by the French army, royalist agitation had been growing. The announcement of a new Constitution, with a law effectively blocking the chance of a royalist majority, provoked strong opposition from the Right. On October 5 (13 Vendémiaire) royalists in Paris rose in rebellion, established an insurrectionary committee and marched on the Tuileries. It was the most formidable challenge the Thermidorian government had yet faced. Government troops were outnumbered by eight to one, the forces which marched against them were the best-organised yet.

Barras was put in command of tne government troops, but it was his appointment of the young Napoleon Bonaparte, who with his famous "whiff of grapeshot" dispersed the rebels, which saved the day for the Convention. Though Barras, in his speech to the Convention, following the victory of 13 Vendémiaire, made only one reference to Napoleon's part in events, there was no doubt, in the public mind, who was the hero of the day. As General Vendémiaire, Napoleon shot from obscurity to fame almost overnight.

Wisely pursuing a policy of moderation, the government took few reprisals after 13 Vendémiaire. But a decree ordering the surrender of all unauthorised arms to the authorities was issued as a precaution shortly after. Hortense de Beauharnais, in her memoirs, describes how her brother Eugène, indignant at the order that he should give up his father's sword, went to see General Bonaparte to ask that he should be allowed to keep it. Bonaparte was touched by his request and agreed. A few days later Joséphine de Beauharnais came to thank him in person. It was the start of their relationship.

Barras, still Joséphine's lover at the time, dismissed the story in his memoirs as romantic fiction. He had no love for his former mistress whose husband, Bonaparte, had thrust him aside on his accession to power. Joséphine, he wrote, had an insatiable love for luxury and money – "she would have drunk gold out of her lover's skull"; her beauty, already fading at the time she first met Bonaparte, "owed everything to art, as calculated, refined and perfected as ever harlots of Greece or Paris employed in their profession".

Bonaparte, timid and inexperienced with women, was instantly seduced. "Madame de Beauharnais was the first woman to give me any degree of confidence," he said in Saint Helena. " . . . One day when I was sitting next to her at table she began to pay me all manner of compliments on my military qualities. Her praise intoxicated me. From that moment I confined my conversation to her and never left her side. I was passionately in love with her and our friends were aware of it long before I ever dared to say a word about it."

Joséphine was not in love with this ardent young man, pale, lank haired and intense. It was only after long inner struggles, she told a friend much later, that she decided to marry him. But she sensed in him qualities far different from those of the corrupt and decadent circle in which she moved. Barras was tiring of her. His newest flame, though not his only one, was Thérésia Tallien. She was already detaching herself from Tallien, whom she would later divorce. The newspapers, referring to her many love affairs, had christened her National Property; the image of Notre Dame de Thermidor was receding fast.

Joséphine bore no grudge against Thérésia, and the two women would continue to be friends and allies till Napoleon, when he came to power, forebade her to appear at court. He was determined to break with the dissolute morals of the preceding era. Thérésia was too closely associated with them to be acceptable. "I forbid you to see Madame Tallien under any pretext whatsoever," he told his wife. " . . . She was once an attractive baggage, she has become a woman of infamy."

Joséphine, at the time of her marriage to Bonaparte, had been on little firmer ground than Madame Tallien. Eight years older than him, with a reputation dubious even for those racy times, she was far from being an obvious match. But she remained incomparable in his eyes. It was a catch phrase of his that *"rien ne valait Joséphine"* – "nothing equalled Joséphine"; the elegance, charm and grace of manner which were to become a legend outweighed all other defects. Barras, in his memoirs, claims that he had offered Bonaparte the command of the army of Italy as a reward for taking Joséphine off his hands. Bonaparte needed no reward. He was madly in love. He had won the command, not through Barras' influence, but on the strength of his own merits.

On March 9, 1796, despite hesitations on Joséphine's side, the marriage between her and Bonaparte took place. Madame Tallien was among the witnesses; the bridegroom was two hours late for the ceremony. Absorbed in his preparations for the Italian campaign he had forgotten the time. The honeymoon lasted only two days; their love affair had been consummated some time before. Bonaparte set off for Italy and the victories that would lead him to glory and a throne. The military dictatorship envisaged by Madame de Staël lay not far ahead. The Revolution, with its tragedies and triumphs, its broken hopes and high ideals, was effectively at an end.

Afterwards

Joséphine de Beauharnais
The opening years of Joséphine's marriage were stormy. Driven to desperation by her infidelity during his absences in Italy and Egypt, Napoleon threatened divorce. They were reconciled after his return to Paris in October 1799. A few weeks later, after the coup of 18 Brumaire, Napoleon became First Consul. Joséphine was crowned Empress by his side in 1804. In 1809, on the grounds of her inability to provide an heir, Napoleon divorced her in order to remarry. She died at Malmaison, her country house near Paris, in 1814.

Madame de la Tour du Pin
Madame de la Tour du Pin and her family arrived in Boston on May 12, 1794. They spent three happy years in America, farming in the remote countryside – Madame de la Tour du Pin's pats of butter, stamped with the family monogram, were much in demand. They returned to France briefly under the Directoire, but were forced to emigrate again, this time to England, until 1800. M. de la Tour du Pin became Minister to the Court in le Hague under Napoleon, then continued to serve his country as a diplomat, first in Holland, then in Italy, under Louis XVIII. He died in 1837. His wife survived him till 1853. Her memoirs, the *Journal d'une Femme du 50 Ans*, begun in 1820, tell the story of her life from childhood till the first year of the Restoration. They were published by her great grandson in 1906.

Madame de Staël

After a brief absence from Paris, Madame de Staël returned there in May 1797, with her lover Benjamin Constant, and was soon in the thick of political intriguing once more. She was expelled by the Directoire in July 1799, but was back in Paris again following Napoleon's coup d'état of November 9 (18 Brumaire). Her political activities and opposition to Napoleon led to her renewed expulsion from Paris in 1802. She remained in exile till Napoleon's abdication in 1814. During this period she published her novels, *Delphine* and *Corinne*, and began her *Considérations sur les Principaux Evénements de la Révolution française*. She died in Paris in 1818.

Madame Tallien

Madame Tallien obtained a divorce from Tallien in 1802. She had long since tired of him, moving on from Barras to become the mistress of the rich speculator Ouvrard, to whom she bore four children. Ostracised from court by Napoleon, she re-established her social position to some extent by her marriage to the Comte de Caraman, later Prince de Chimay. The marriage was long and happy and she passed the later years of her life on the family estates at Chimay, surrounded by her numerous children. Meanwhile Tallien, after a period as consul in Alicante, had returned to Paris, an impoverished and discredited figure. He died in poverty in 1820. Madame Tallien survived him till 1835.

Select Bibliography

Abrantès, Duchesse d', *Mémoires*, Paris, 1831

Abray, Jane, "Feminism in the French Revolution", American Historical Review, February 1975

Almeras, Henri d', *Barras et son Temps*, Albin Michel, 1930

Aulard, Alphonse, "Le féminisme pendant la Révolution française", Revue Bleue, 4th ser., 9, pp. 362–366, 1898

Balayé, Simone, *Madame de Staël*, Editions Klinckseick, 1979

Barras, Vicomte de, *Mémoires*, ed. G. Duruy, Paris, 1896

Bertaut, Jules, *Madame Tallien*, Arthème Fayard, 1954

Beugnot, Count, *Life and Adventures*, ed. C. M. Yonge, London, 1871

Bienvenu, J. (ed.) *The Ninth of Thermidor*, Oxford University Press, 1968

Blanc, Olivier, *Olympe de Gouges*, Syros, 1981

Blennerhassett, Lady, *Madame de Staël*, London 1889

Bouloiseau, Marc, *The Jacobin Republic*, trans. J. Mandelbaum, Cambridge University Press, 1983

Brusson, Ferdinand, *Condorcet*, Félix Alcan, 1929

Castelnau, Jules, *Madame Tallien*, Hachette, 1938

Carlyle, Thomas, *The French Revolution*, London, 1839

Castelot, André, *Joséphine*, Marabout, 1967

Chimay, Princesse de, *Madame Tallien*, Plon, 1936

Clémenceau-Jacquemaire, Madeleine, *Vie de Madame Roland*, Jules Tallandier, 1929

Cobban, Alfred, *Aspects of the French Revolution*, Jonathan Cape, 1968

Cole, H., *Josephine*, Heinemann, 1962

Condorcet, *Oeuvres*, ed. F. O'Connor and M. F. Arago, Paris, 1848

Dauban, C. A., *Etude sur Madame Roland et son Temps*, Paris, 1864

Diesbach, Ghislain de, *Madame de Staël*, Perrin, 1983

Ducrest, G., *Memoirs of the Empress Josephine*, trs. H. S. Nichols, London, 1894

Duhet, Paule-Marie (ed.) *Cahiers des Doléances des Femmes*, Paris, 1981

Duhet, Paule-Marie, *Les Femmes et la Révolution, 1789–1794*, Julliard, 1971

Ernst, Otto, *Théroigne de Méricourt*, Payot, 1935

Furet, F. and Richet, D., *La Révolution Française*, 1979, Marabout

Gastine, J. L., *La Belle Tallien, Notre Dame de Septembre*, Paris, 1909

Gastine, J. L., *Reine du Directoire, Madame Tallien*, Paris, 1908

Gilchrist, J. and Murray, W. J., (ed.) *The Press in the French Revolution*, Cheshire Gunn, 1977

Goncourt, Edmond and Jules de, *Histoire de la Société Française pendant la Révolution*, Paris, 1854

Goncourt, Edmond and Jules de, *Histoire de la Société Française pendant le Directoire*, Paris, 1899

Herold, J. Christopher, *Mistress to an Age*, Hamish Hamilton, 1959

Hibbert, Christopher, *The French Revolution*, Allen Lane, 1959

Hortense, Queen, *Mémoires*, Paris, 1927

Houssaye, Arsène, *Notre Dame de Thermidor*, Paris, 1867

Hufton, Olwen, "Women in Revolution, 1789–1796", Past and Present, November, 1971

Knapton, E. J., *Empress Josephine*, Harvard University Press, 1964

La Tour du Pin, Marquise de, *Journal d'une Femme de 50 Ans*, Berger-Levrault, 1954

La Tour du Pin, Marquise de, *Memoirs of Madame de la Tour du Pin*, ed. and trans. Félice Harcourt, Harvill, 1969

Lacour, Léopold, *Trois Femmes de la Révolution*, Paris, 1900

Laing, Margaret, *Josephine and Napoleon*, Sidgwick and Jackson, 1973

Lamartine, Alphonse de, *Histoire des Girondins*, Brussels, 1847

Lenotre, G., *Vieilles Maisons, Vieux Papiers*, Paris, 1919

Lenotre, G., *Paris Révolutionnaire*, Paris, 1916

Lefèbvre, G., *The French Revolution: From its origins to 1793*, trans. E. Moss Evanson, Routledge and Kegan Paul, 1962

Levy, D., Applewhite, H. B., Johnson, M. D., (ed.) *Women in Revolutionary Paris*, University of Illinois Press, 1979

Loomis, Stanley, *Paris in the Terror*, Jonathan Cape, 1964

Marcourt, André de, *La Véritable Madame Tallien*, Des Portiques, 1933

Markham, Felix, *Napoleon*, Weidenfeld and Nicolson, 1963

Matrat, Jean, *Robespierre*, trans. F. Brenner, Angus & Robertson, 1975

May, Gita, *Madame Roland and the Age of Revolution*, Columbia University Press, 1970

Melchior-Bonnet, Bernardine, *Les Girondins*, Perrin, 1969

Mercier, L. S., *Nouveau Paris*, Paris, 1797

Michelet, J., *Histoire de la Révolution Française*, Levasseur, 1933
Michelet, J., *Les Femmes de la Révolution*, Paris, 1854
Morris, Gouverneur, *A Diary of the French Revolution*, ed. Beatrix Cary
    Davenport, Harrap, 1939
Pasquier, Chancelier, *Souvenirs*, Hachette, 1964
Pellet, Marcellin, *Théroigne de Méricourt*, Paris, 1902
Roberts, J. M., *The French Revolution*, Oxford University Press, 1978
Roland, Madame, *Mémoires*, ed. Claude Perroud, Paris 1905
Salvameni, Gaetano, *The French Revolution, 1788–1792*, trans. I. M.
    Rawson, Jonathan Cape, 1965
Seward, Desmond, *Marie Antoinette*, Constable, 1981
Shearing, Joseph, *The Angel of the Assassination*, Heinemann, 1935
Sonolet, Louis, *Madame Tallien*, Paris, 1909
Staël, Madame de, *Correspondance Générale*, vols II i and ii, ed. Beatrice
    W. Jasinski, Jean-Jacques Pauvert, 1960
Staël, Madame de, *Considérations sur les Principaux Evénements de la
    Révolution Française*, Paris, 1818
Stephens, Winifred, *Women of the French Revolution*, Chapman and Hall,
    1922
Strobl von Ravelsberg, F., *Les Confessions de Théroigne de Méricourt*, Paris,
    1892
Sydenham, M. J.; *The Girondins*, Athlone Press, 1961
Tannahill, Reay, *Paris in the Revolution*, Folio Society, 1966
Thompson, J. M., *The French Revolution*, Basil Blackwell, 1943
Tomalin, Claire, *Mary Wollstonecraft*, Weidenfeld and Nicolson, 1974
Wilson, R. McNair, *Josephine*, Eyre and Spottiswode, 1930
Wilson, R. McNair, *Gipsy Queen of Paris, Madame Tallien*, Chapman &
    Hall, 1934

Index

HAMISH HAMILTON PAPERBACKS

'Among the most collectable of paperback imprints . . .'
Christopher Hudson, *The Standard*

All books in the Hamish Hamilton Paperback Series are available at your
local bookshop or can be ordered by post. A full list of titles and an order
form can be found at the end of this book.

NANCY MITFORD
A Memoir

Harold Acton

Nancy Mitford never completed an autobiography. Fortunately she was a voluminous letter writer and had a genius for friendship and laughter. In this delightful memoir, Sir Harold Acton has been able to show us, largely in her own words, almost every aspect of her personality, and her immense courage during the years of her final painful illness.

'Sir Harold Acton has memoralised a very gifted writer, and a unique personality, with affection, skill and truth.' Anthony Powell, *Daily Telegraph*

'The main lesson I derived from Sir Harold's stylish and loving evocation of Nancy Mitford's personality, is that she gave just as much pleasure to her circle of friends and relations as she gave to her readers.' Antonia Fraser, *Evening Standard*

MEMOIRS OF AN AESTHETE

Harold Acton

In this outstanding memoir, deservedly regarded as a classic, Harold Acton writes a witty and vivid account of the first thirty-five years of his life from his boyhood among the international colony of dilettanti in Florence before the First World War, to his maturity when he discovered his spiritual home in Peking before the old Chinese culture was destroyed by Chairman Mao.

'He is a connoisseur of language. . . . His prose scintillates. It reminds one of Beerbohm and Waugh.' Patrick Skene Catling

'A truly magical memoir.' Linda O'Callaghan, *Sunday Telegraph*

JOHN MASEFIELD
A Life

Constance Babington Smith

John Masefield's early life hardly held the promise of his eventual achievement. Apprenticed in 1894, aged fifteen, to a merchant sailing ship, he acquired a love of the sea but not the stamina to continue as a sailor, then he worked his way in the United States for two years until he returned to England determined to become a writer; after many struggles he gained the literary recognition he deserved. Finally came his appointment to the Poet Laureateship in 1930. Drawing on a mass of archive material including Masefield's multitudinous letters, Constance Babington Smith brings vividly to life the man whose mild and unassuming manner belied his outstanding powers as a writer.

'Miss Babington Smith is a sympathetic, yet objective observer, and through her work shine out clearly those qualities of Masefield noted by Sir John Betjeman . . . his kindness, his goodness, above all his modesty.' T. J. Binyon, *Times Literary Supplement*

I LEAP OVER THE WALL

Monica Baldwin
Introduction by Karen Armstrong

In 1914, on her twenty-first birthday, Monica Baldwin entered one of the oldest and most strictly enclosed contemplative orders of the Roman Catholic Church. Twenty-eight years later, after having obtained a special rescript from Rome dispensing her from her vows, she left with her faith in her religion and her respect for monastic life intact; but it had taken her many years to discover that she herself had not the true vocation for the religious life. Interwoven with her witty accounts of the problems she had to tackle on her return to the outside world are descriptions of convent life. Miss Baldwin makes one understand that the severe discipline is spiritually worth while and can be totally fulfilling. This is a book which no one can read without being the richer for it.

'What a wonderful book! Now that I have finished it, I want to read it again . . . Whatever you think about nuns, whatever your religious views or lack of them, I don't see how you can fail to be enriched by this book.' John Betjeman, *Daily Herald*

IN THE CANNON'S MOUTH

P. J. Campbell

'A remarkable power of recollection informs Campbell's personal story of the First World War . . . his account of that time is as fresh and vivid as if it were yesterday.' *Sunday Times*

'The outward simplicity of his style conceals a great deal of art and intensity of feeling . . . This is an honest, direct book . . . It can stand as an image for the many millions of men trapped in the darkness of that war.' *Economist*

MISSION WITH MOUNTBATTEN

Alan Campbell-Johnson

From 1947 until June 1948 Alan Campbell-Johnson was Lord Mountbatten's Press Attaché in India. The diary he kept of those dramatic and critical months was the first authoritative account to be published of one of the most important events of this century: the transfer of power in India by partition and consent. Both for those who remember that crucial time and for a new generation, this remarkable book provides a fascinating view of statesmanship at its most creative.

'A most revealing and graphic report of one of the most extraordinary and imaginative episodes in our history.' Arthur Bryant

ANOTHER PART OF THE WOOD
A Self Portrait

Kenneth Clark

Kenneth Clark's sharp witty account of his eccentric Edwardian upbringing and his swift success in the world of art after leaving Oxford is a classic of its kind and a pleasure to read.

'An immensely entertaining memoir . . . rich in deliciously dry tales . . . all told with perfect brevity and wit.' Michael Ratcliffe, *The Times*

'A dispassionate record of his reverses and his triumphs. His astringent, worldly humour increases the book's charm.' Peter Quennell, *Listener*

THE OTHER HALF
A Self Portrait

Kenneth Clark

With this sequel to *Another Part of the Wood* Kenneth Clark continues the classic account of his life from the outbreak of the Second World War to his outstanding achievement as presenter of the TV series *Civilisation*.

'What is most delightful in the book is the series of portraits of his friends and one or two of his enemies. . . . Lord Clark has a curiously waspish turn of phrase which brings out the faults of those whose memory he cherishes and makes them seem far more real.' David Holloway, *Daily Telegraph*

'His style remains sparely elegant, his mood self-deprecating, his affections touched with malice. . . . There is, however, nothing small or mean about Lord Clark, least of all in his friendships.' Kenneth Rose, *Sunday Telegraph*

THE 'IT' GIRLS

Meredith Etherington-Smith and Jeremy Pilcher

The story of two extraordinary sisters – Elinor Glyn, the most notorious novelist of her time, particularly remembered for her society-shocker *Three Weeks*; and Lucy Duff-Gordon, the dazzling couturiere 'Lucile' who revolutionised dress design in late Victorian and Edwardian England, building up highly successful businesses in London, Paris and the U.S.A.

'Brave, independent, pioneering New Women of an unconventional breed . . . their biographers have done them proud.' Hilary Spurling, *Observer*

'They were women of phenomenal energy, who lived their lives to the full and to a good old age. They both, also, had great talent. . . . I enjoyed it greatly.' Susan Hill, *Good Housekeeping*

THE DIARY OF AN ART DEALER

René Gimpel

In this diary, René Gimpel, one of the great international art dealers of his day, describes the world of art during the years 1918 to 1939, and, more importantly, the people involved in it. Artists, collectors, colleagues, art critics, and others such as Proust, are scrutinized with affection and wit, and their personalities and eccentricities caught in vivid anecdotes.

'A journal of much the same literary quality and historical value as the Duc de Saint-Simon's classical memoirs . . . René Gimpel will be read with enjoyment when the journals of André Gide or Albert Camus have been forgotten by all but a few scholars.' Edouard Roditi, *New York Times Book Review*

BEYOND FRONTIERS

Jasper Parrott with Vladimir Ashkenazy

Vladimir Ashkenazy is known throughout the world as one of the greatest pianists of our time. Despite his fame he is a very private man, but his experiences as a child prodigy under the Soviet system and his subsequent emigration to the West have affected so profoundly his views about music, politics and people that this book has grown out of his wish to share these thoughts with others – to communicate in a medium other than music.

'. . . a far cry from the usual collection of amiable anecdotes surrounding the life of a virtuoso. Instead, it is an examination of the thoughts, musical and political, of a great artist, written with intelligence, wit, and even wisdom.' André Previn

MRS PAT
The Life of Mrs. Patrick Campbell

Margot Peters

Beautiful, witty, talented, Mrs. Patrick Campbell became a legend in her own lifetime. Her theatrical career encompassed tremendous triumphs and unmitigated failures. Her private life was controversial and tragic. In this superb biography Margot Peters captures the magnetism of an outstanding actress and extraordinary woman, who remains today as intriguing as ever.

'The book has been researched with exemplary care and accuracy. The famous bons mots – nearly always witty, sometimes cruel and personal, but usually devastatingly apt – are quoted with appropriate relish. There is a wealth of material, never before made public, to enthrall the reader.' John Gielgud, *Observer*

BISMARCK
THE MAN AND THE STATESMAN

A. J. P. Taylor

In this outstanding biography, A. J. P. Taylor discusses not only Bismarck's political ideas and achievements but also his strange complicated character. It is a fascinating essay on the psychology as well as the political understanding of a man who remains to this day a subject of controversy.

'Rich, learned, profound and yet highly readable . . . Mr Taylor has written many good books. This is the best.' Hugh Trevor-Roper, *Sunday Times*

THE YEARS WITH ROSS

James Thurber

Harold Ross was *The New Yorker*'s brilliant and often eccentric editor from its founding in 1925 until his death in 1951. When James Thurber joined its staff in 1927, he discovered Ross to be a prickly, unpredictable individualist with a rasping voice, unerring taste and a searing passion for facts. He was a disastrous administrator, and his relations with the staff and contributors tended to be stormy, but all admitted that he was an editor of genius. As one reads Thurber's wildly funny account of what went on, one is not so much surprised at the magazine's success as that it ever appeared at all.

'The classic tribute by Ross's most devoted colleague, to the magazine, the eccentrics who gathered round it and above all to its wayward, sometimes monstrous proprietor.' *Sunday Times*

Available in Hamish Hamilton Paperbacks

WALTER SCOTT: HIS LIFE AND PERSONALITY	Hesketh Pearson	£6.95 ☐
THE LETTERS OF EDWIN LUTYENS	eds. Clayre Percy and Jane Ridley	£7.95 ☐
MRS PAT	Margot Peters	£5.95 ☐
THE SECRET ORCHARD OF ROGER ACKERLEY	Diana Petre	£4.95 ☐
THE BONUS OF LAUGHTER★	Alan Pryce-Jones	£6.95 ☐
ALBERT, PRINCE CONSORT	Robert Rhodes James	£4.95 ☐
LORD RANDOLPH CHURCHILL	Robert Rhodes James	£6.95 ☐
MY MANY YEARS★	Arthur Rubinstein	£7.95 ☐
MARY BERENSON	eds. Barbara Strachey and Jayne Samuels	£5.95 ☐
BISMARCK	A. J. P. Taylor	£5.95 ☐
THE YEARS WITH ROSS★	James Thurber	£4.95 ☐
END OF A JOURNEY★	Philip Toynbee	£7.95 ☐
CHEKHOV	Henri Troyat	£6.95 ☐
GLADYS DUCHESS OF MARLBOROUGH	Hugo Vickers	£6.95 ☐
THE DRAGON EMPRESS	Marina Warner	£4.95 ☐
TCHAIKOVSKY★	John Warrack	£6.95 ☐
GEORGE★	Emlyn Williams	£6.95 ☐
THE GREAT HUNGER	Cecil Woodham-Smith	£6.95 ☐
QUEEN VICTORIA	Cecil Woodham-Smith	£5.95 ☐

All titles 198 × 126 mm, and all contain 8 pages of black and white illustrations except for those marked★.

All books in the Hamish Hamilton Paperback Series are available at your local bookshop, or can be ordered direct from J. Barnicoat (Falmouth) Ltd. Just tick the titles you want in the list above and fill in the form below.

Name_____

Address_____

_____

Write to: J. Barnicoat (Falmouth) Ltd, PO Box 11, Falmouth, Cornwall TR10 9EN.

Please enclose cheque or postal order made out to J. Barnicoat (Falmouth) Ltd for the cover price plus postage:

UK: 60p for the first book, 25p for the second book and 15p for each additional book to a maximum of £1.90.

OVERSEAS (including EIRE): £1.25 for the first book, 75p for the second book and 28p for each additional book.

Hamish Hamilton Ltd reserve the right to show new retail prices on covers which may differ from those previously advertised in the text or elsewhere, and to increase postal rates in accordance with the P.O.